The American Funeral

The American Funeral

A Study in Guilt, Extravagance, and Sublimity

By LEROY BOWMAN, Ph. D.

INTRODUCTION BY HARRY A. OVERSTREET

GREENWOOD PRESS, PUBLISHERS
WESTPORT, CONNECTICUT

The Library of Congress has catalogued this publication as follows:

Library of Congress Cataloging in Publication Data

Bowman, Le Roy Edward, 1887–
   The American funeral.

   Includes bibliographical references.
   1. Funeral rites and ceremonies--United States.
I. Title.
[GT3203.B6 1973]   393'.0973   72-14083
ISBN 0-8371-6749-3

Copyright 1959 by Public Affairs Press

Originally published in 1959
by Public Affairs Press, Washington, D. C.

Reprinted with the permission
of Public Affairs Press

First Greenwood Reprinting 1973

Library of Congress Catalogue Card Number 72-14083

ISBN 0-8371-6749-3

Printed in the United States of America

INTRODUCTION

This is a strange and necessary book—strange, because no one voluntarily chooses to talk about funerals, particularly his own; necessary, because the time has come when all of us ought to be talking about the kind of funerals that human dignity would seem to require.

Funerals have not been among the happiest of our human inventions. In fact, they have, in our day, become something about which we are increasingly embarrassed.

Some twenty five years ago, Dr. Bowman tells us, a serious effort was made by a researching mind to change the funeral into a service more commensurate both with the spirit of man and with the high mystery of death. But the effort failed; and no comparable one, he reports, has since been made.

Why did that effort fail? What can we now do to overcome our strange reluctance to think frankly and openly about the ceremonial of death? Above all, how can we rescue the funeral from the pressures of commercialism that make it far too often into a tawdry response to prestige demands?

Curiously enough, there is hardly any major event in life which we are more unprepared to meet than the "disposal" of our friends and loved ones. Mostly we have shied away from the problem; allowed the mortuary professionals to take over. We have seldom been bold or knowledgeable enough to express preferences of our own that go counter to the funerary mores.

I remember one noble old man of our community—a genius in his vocation—who made a compact with his most intimate friend, the minister of his church, that if he should predecease him, his friend would carry his ashes to the ocean beach and scatter them to the winds of heaven. And so it was done. The old man had walked that beach many times; he had heard the whistle of its winds in his ears; and he wanted beach and winds to take him back.

v

Such frank freedom is hardly looked upon with favor either by the legal guardians of our bodies or by the corporations that make plans to take them over for a fee.

Dr. Bowman believes there are things we can do about the ceremonies of death if we set our minds to consider them. We may discover our own preferred ways to say good-by; nor be made ashamed if we say them with simplicity.

HARRY A. OVERSTREET

Falls Church, Virginia

PREFACE

In its secular aspects the American funeral appears to be an anachronism, an elaboration of early customs rather than the adaptation to modern needs that it should be. Properly employed, it is a highly useful and essential function of society. Improperly used it deteriorates into little more than a shabby opportunity for an undertaker to exploit and sometimes impoverish bereaved families.

Against protests over the lavish display of expensive caskets and the multitude of costly floral decorations to be seen at most final rites, the funeral directors raise their voices to proclaim the lasting satisfaction they furnish their customers. Bereaved families, they point with pride and some justification, need solace regardless of price. Moreover, they contend, the social status and prestige of sorrowing survivors must be proclaimed by appearances at the funeral.

Invariably the burden of popular magazine articles on the American funeral is the high cost of dying. A much broader approach is taken in these pages.

The purpose of this study is to acquaint the reader with the basis of charges of commercial exploitation directed at undertakers, to ascertain what peculiar circumstances influence the methods he uses, and to uncover the social and psychological factors that underlie conspicuous display. While religious aspects of the funeral are taken into account, they are not dealt with in detail since they are the subject of many books.

In essence, this study is intended to fill the gap left by the social scientists who have neglected or disregarded the funeral. The reasons for their behavior and the attitude of the ordinary citizen can best be explained in terms of the cultural proscriptions bearing on death.

Although anthropologists assign a positive function to the rite in primitive societies, no serious scientific effort has been made to ascertain whether a like function is served by the funeral in modern industrialized society.

The research for this study was carried on over a period of five years. It involved innumerable first-hand observations of funerals and the activities connected with them; hundreds of interviews with undertakers, members of bereaved families, clergymen, physicians, nurses, social workers, and government officials; interpretation and tabulation of 400 responses to a questionnaire; the reading of histories, magazine articles, news items, novels, and manuals for funeral directors and clergymen as well as analysis of the legal aspects of the subject. First-hand observation of a score of actual funerals and interviews with all the main participants proved to be the most rewarding method.

Four days to two weeks were spent in each of two small villages, in two towns of approximately 5,000 inhabitants, in two cities of 185,000 and 340,000 population, in three metropolitan areas of over 1,000,000 each, in two suburbs, and in neighborhoods of several large cities. Over one hundred group discussions on the subject were held.

A brief note on terminology needs to be made. The three terms "funeral director," "undertaker," and "mortician" are used interchangeably in these pages. Currently leading practitioners are attempting to get "funeral director" into general usage. However, the term "undertaker" is used for the most part by the rank and file of the trade and by the public. "Mortician" is sometimes used.

Preceding Parts II and III are explanatory statements designed to be introductory to the chapters in these parts. These statements deserve particular attention in that they point up the special significance of the chapters that follow. However, for the sake of physical uniformity they are given chapter treatment.

To appraise the function of the modern funeral, a philosophical approach has been taken in the last chapter, contrasting with the strictly scientific approach of the preceding material.

Thanks are due for the help of many persons, but most particularly to Professor Robert K. Merton, of the Sociology Department of Columbia University, for his invaluable counsel in the early part of the study; to Garda W. Bowman for unfailing help in many ways; and to Mrs. Joy Shostak for much time spent in laborious tabulating. Gratitude is also due officers of many public and private agencies who furnished helpful information.

LeRoy Bowman

Brooklyn, N. Y.

CONTENTS

PART I: STAGE SETTING AND PERFORMANCE

I
A Wilderness of Attitudes   1

II
Death Strikes the Family   8

III
Group Behavior at Funeral Gatherings   16

PART II: THE FUNERAL BUSINESS

IV
"Behind the Scenes"   27

V
The Bargaining Situation: Family and Undertaker   29

VI
Institutional Relationships   55

VII
The Undertaker's Role in the Community   71

VIII
Dominance of Commercial Factors   89

PART III: CHANGES IN FORMS AND FUNCTIONS

IX
Approach to Cultural Change   109

X
Effects of City Civilization   112

XI
Trends and Experiments   129

PART IV: OVERVIEW

Meanings and Meaningful Funerals   140

Appendices   161
References   176
Index   180

PART I

STAGE SETTING AND PERFORMANCE

CHAPTER I

A WILDERNESS OF ATTITUDES

We have given the world our passion,
We have naught for death but toys.
WILLIAM BUTLER YEATS

Funerals in the United States are the objects of a wide variety of emotional reactions, frequently contradictory as between different individuals, and not infrequently inconsistent for the same individual on different occasions. Often reactions to funerals reflect the attitudes toward death and dead bodies; and these attitudes, in turn, are as diverse as horror and amusement. To discuss funerals is not the proper thing to do in some social circles, and yet the subject is of considerable interest.

It will be of help in reading the pages that follow if there is some understanding of the 'anomalies in the reactions to funerals. At the same time insight may also be gained into a circumstance of funerals that needs explanation. It is the failure on the part of leaders of institutions to give any but the most cursory attention to an analysis of the functioning of funerals in society. Even the social scientists have failed to do much more than classify funeral usages among rites and rituals after explaining the general significance of all ceremonies. Funerals have occurred continually and universally; the high and the low arrange them for their dead and attend those held for relatives, friends and associates. Why are they taken as a matter of course without an evaluation of their worth or the adequacy of the manner in which their non-religious aspects are conducted? As nation, and as states and communities, we are a daring people when it comes to change. We pride ourselves on progress, and on being strictly up to date—except for a few matters that slip by unobserved and neglected. Prominent among them is the funeral. No one can list with finality the reasons for the lack of interest and action in this

1

matter. However, there are reasons which at least furnish clues to an explanation.

Urban Evasion of Evidences of Death. The comprehensive cause which underlies the lack of attention to death and funerals lies in the fact that urbanites, and increasingly ruralites, are seldom brought face to face with death and the evidences of death. This was not true in the early stages of American history. Living on farms, as a much larger proportion of families did in former generations, brought young and old closer to the cycle of birth, life and death of animals. They were slaughtered or they died from natural causes before the eyes of everyone. Bodies of animals and even of members of the family were often given burial on the farms. The sick and the aged resided then in the homes; today a large number die in hospitals and not a few in homes for the aged.

The inadequacy in modern city life of opportunity for children to learn by experience how to deal with animal bodies is illustrated in the not unusual incident that happened to one young girl. When her beloved rabbit died she became disconsolate over the disposition of the body. The proposal to bury it in the back yard (a possibility seldom available to city dwellers) brought a storm of protest because it might be dug up by dogs. There was no place to bury it except in an expensive plot in a dog cemetery forty miles away. For the first time her parents realized the need of animal cemeteries they had ridiculed before their predicament. They thought of hospitals for cats and, after discovering the term in the classified telephone directory was "dog and cat" hospital, arranged with one of them for a fee of three dollars to accept "for burial" the small body, wrapped tenderly in tissue paper and enclosed in an elaborate box tied with red ribbon. The procedure satisfied the girl. Even so there was no chance for her to see her pet buried with whatever observance she might think proper.

Caring for the remains of close relatives, or of non-relatives living near by, was in former generations a responsibility first of the family members, or, failing that, of neighbors. There are older persons now living who can remember instances in which a mother anticipating death has asked her daughter to bathe and dress her for the funeral. In the habits of families and in the customs of communities death was a reality to be adjusted to and funerals were occasions in which all participated. There were well-known modes of behavior for such occasions. There were discrepancies among funerals to be sure, but there were recognized rules to go by and most persons abided by them.

The coffin was carried to the grave or put into a carriage by rela-tives, friends and neighbors. Often it was buried in the church yard where the reminders of the dead of the community's past were plainly evident to the living. The religion of life was preached within a few feet of the "relicts" of previous generations.

Today we live more and more out of sight, or even understanding, of death of the animals whose flesh we eat. A visit to a slaughter-house is for the majority of persons an awful experience. Our sick and old are living in larger numbers outside the home and care of relatives, and in much larger numbers dying under the methodical supervision of nurses, physicians and other professionals. Grave-yards are not near the churches, nor in neighborhoods, but in an out-lying cemetery belt around the city. They are forbidden by ordinance within the limits of most of the larger municipalities. There is al-most complete absence of a community feeling when a mourner visits the grave of a relative or neighbor in a vast expanse of tombstones.

Bodies do not even lie in the homes before burial, but, as a rule, are taken immediately after death to the funeral parlor. Moments or, at the most, a very few hours after a father, son or brother has died, everything about him has become unfamiliar—the clothes he wears, the bed which encases him, the room and the building in which his body waits for burial.

Because of the avoidance of the sight or thought of death, and de-spite the knowledge that it occurs about us constantly, we as a people have not developed rational attitudes toward it nor logical means of dealing with it. The failure of city dwellers to become acquainted with the reality of death, and the absence of the need to deal actively with it, result in an attitude of passivity when it does present itself. Inexperience begets uncertainty and incompetence; and they, in turn, beget a willingness to let someone else meet the issue. The family or the individual responsible for the formal recognition of its dead mem-ber has little basis of judgment on the purpose and value of the occa-sion, and as a consequence readily follows the suggestions of the only expert he knows about, the funeral director.

Escapist Attitudes. Lack of attention breeds indifference, a very common attitude of men and women toward funerals. Indifference, in turn, explains in part why funerals exist in a mass of conflicting re-actions. Such an attitude is not altogether illogical, however, under the crcumstances of city life, as can be seen when the individual is questioned about his lack of forethought for his own last two or three days above the earth. Ofter he answers that it is none of his concern, "I won't know what is going on, nor care what they do with me." All of which is true, but all of which also ignores the place one life has in the lives and loves of others, and the work of the world. However, if the indifferent individual is covering up a need to be recognized in life and a sense of futility in a ceremonial aftermath of life, he is pointing a skeptical finger at a phase of modern society that has great bearing on the meaning of funerals today.

Indifference to the subject may be, on the other hand, a defensive, surface reaction to a deep lying desire to avoid speaking of the subject for fear of exhibiting emotion. It is almost taboo in the United States to show feeling of any depth, especially of sorrow. The same tendency to avoid the subject is illustrated in the impropriety of mentioning it in plain language. In certain circles if it becomes necessary to speak of death only brief references are made and even then the use of direct terms is avoided. In such circles no one ever dies; the proper procedure is to "pass away," or "expire."

The opposite of the avoidance of funerals is also found. Some persons need to express a sort of unfocused sorrow and enjoy having their tears stimulated by funerals. The fact is attested by the few but persistent ones who attend many funerals, often of individuals known slightly or not at all. On occasion these few are the only ones who weep audibly during the funeral service. When he was the warden of St. Stephens College, the Reverend Doctor Bernard Iddings Bell declared in a sermon:

"We modern people are to an extraordinary degree sentimental about death. By a conspiracy of silence and pretense we attempt to forget its inevitability. We make our funerals as unlike funerals as possible. . . . I have even seen the faces of corpses rouged.

"All this is macabre, morbid, indecent. We try to avoid even the mortuary word. People 'pass on' or 'pass away' or 'go west,' everything save plain 'die.' "

In the course of gathering material on the funeral I encountered many persons in positions in which the subject might be expected to come up at least occasionally; most informed me that they seldom, if ever, participated in any discussions involving the subject. Two typical instances will illustrate. The executive of a ministerial association in a large city of "up-state" New York reported that he never heard a discussion of funerals among ministers or laymen. The director of a large social center in a city of considerable size told me that he had not talked about funerals as the main topic of conversation before he engaged with me in such a discussion for an evening. Then it was disclosed that he was thoroughly conversant with the norms of the various social groups in the community as they involved death and burial, and the psycho-social, as well as the economic problems involved.

It is a matter not merely of neglect of the subject, but of resistance, often emotional, to any attempt to consider it. In a group the introduction of the subject may arouse resistance of one or a few individuals and occasionally of the great majority of the members. Typically, a man or a woman protests without provocation, "I don't worry about death. I am happy and don't let myself think about it. Everyone says I am cheerful. I surely don't fear death." Even counselors with professional training may declare that it is a mistake to pay any attention to death; life is the thing to think about. The same position, essentially, was taken by a number of respondents to a questionnaire. They inquired about the purpose of the study further than had been explained, and expressed the conviction that no constructive purpose could be served by spending time on the subject. More than a few retaliated against the broaching of the subject by indicating that only a morbid or humorous interest could inspire the questions. Despite these defensive reactions, in every one of many groups in which the subject has been broached there has followed an animated discussion of it.

The behavior of groups as they discuss funerals, funeral directors, death, corpses and the dying is as unpredictable and seemingly irrational as any of the many curious aspects of this subject. In tone, the discussions range from the sublime to the ribald, with the accent resting heavily on the latter. This sort of difference in treatment of the subject might be expected, perhaps, as between the groups of less and the groups of more breeding, or as between the less educated and the intellectually highly trained. But the fact is that the cultured and well educated become as hilarious as any one over the rather non-humorous matter of the individual's leaving this life. It seems that when the occasion is close in point of time to the death of a loved one the discussant is inclined to regard the subject in its sublime light. When the company includes no one who has had a recent experience of the kind, the whole group is as likely as not to accept the introduction of the subject as a cue for hilarity. This applies at least to some of the adherents of each of the three major faiths, those of great as well as less seriousness in their religious convictions.

The element of suppression, for one thing, lends a sense of hilarity, if not humor, to the subject for certain groups of people. They have a good time breaking through the barriers of inhibition against the discussion of the frowned upon topics. The topic is very much like that of sex in this respect, and it must furnish a welcome change from discussion of sex for some of those who have over played the one topic and yet who need frequently to let down the bars of propriety. The fact that discussion of death and funerals occurs less frequently than discussion of sex must add to the sense of release when it is brought up.

Repression probably operates on these occasions in another fashion for many individuals. The subject most certainly arouses a sense of personal identification with death on the part of a large number of men and women, and some measure of realization of its inevitability for them. The accompanying fear, or at the very least uneasiness, would lead quickly to a defensive mask, behind which the individuals experiencing it could hope to deceive themselves and other persons present. The ribaldry goes the lengths it does because no criterion of good taste on the subject has been built into the conversational habits of the individuals by previous experience.

The Reverend Dr. James A. Pike, former Dean of the Cathedral of St. John the Divine in New York City, characterized the modern attitude toward death as being "something we do not wish to face so we either laugh at it, as we would at an incongruity, or bury it in the recesses of our minds." As a matter of fact, incongruity is a large factor in the ribaldry that can be observed in the reaction of some groups to the subject of death, or to the dead body at the most extreme form of wakes. I have witnessed it also in the interchange between men who handle bodies outside the context of funerals. The body is like a human being in appearance but not in action. Its lack of response is incongruous with the expectations one has of a human being. Then, too, it does not react to stimuli in the environment around it, and that fact may add a sense of superiority to the onlookers who regard the body superciliously. On sober second thought it is difficult to see incongruity in the remains of any human being, unless death itself is an incongruity rather than a normal reality to be faced.

Just as avoidance of the subject of death and of evidences of it leads

to passivity in the event of death, so the defensive and escapist tendencies in the reactions of large numbers of persons lead to excesses of
behavior when death occurs. The underlying, if subconscious, urge
is the same: forgetfulness of the fact, or escape from consideration of
the meaning of death to the surviving individuals. In the hours immediately succeeding the last heart beat of a man or woman, those
closest to him in life show one other escapist tendency, partly on the
basis of which has been constructed much of the dragged out procedure of the modern funeral. It is the reluctance to separate from
the carnal remains at the same time that aversion to the dead body is
experienced. The ambivalence of the wife or husband, son or daughter is in part due to the absence in modern urban culture of experiences of dealing with death in any form, and of rational consideration
of them.

In this welter of attitudes in the community toward it, attitudes
sober and supercilious, critical and unthinking, sympathetic and unfeeling, death comes to families unprepared to meet its tragic consequences.

Chapter II

DEATH STRIKES THE FAMILY

Wherefore all these last offices and ceremonies that concern the dead,
the careful funeral arrangements, and the equipment of the tomb,
and the pomp of obsequies, are rather the solace of the living than
the comfort of the dead.

Saint Augustine

Death strikes its most awful blow to the hearts and minds of those
whose association has been most intimate and continuous with the
person whose life has been snuffed out. All the defensive attitudes
that may have been built up against its coming, all the rationalizations in which any one may have indulged about its inevitability—
these are paper armor when the fatal hour comes. Philosophy and
faith may help to meet the crisis; they are, however, but ways of cop-
ing with it; the happening itself is tragedy. Death may be long in
coming because of prolonged sickness or lengthened weaknesses of old
age, until the final going is shorn of its most tragic features. Even
so, the dragging months of illness or senility have simply borrowed
the bigger part of death's calamity, slowly to dole it out until the
final payment has been made.

Family Disorganization and Bereavement. The consequences of
death bear upon the members of the surviving community in relative
degrees, burdening most heavily the persons who have been most
closely connected with the deceased, and affecting in less and less
measure those whose relationships were less intimate. At the outer-
most edge of the web of relationships, those with whom the deceased
had least to do, and those whose interests his life merely touched, may
scarcely be aware of the occurrence. One student of bereavement
makes clear the distinction between its major effect in the family and
its lesser forms of deprivation upon those outside the family:

"Outside of primary groups—in the sense of groups involving affective attachments—one does not find bereavement in any true sense.
Outside the circle of personal acquaintance one may experience degrees of "shock" depending upon one's capacities for one or another
type of identification and sympathy, or upon the existence of other

than affectional interests or habits disturbed by death. One may also observe rituals and simulations of bereavement, required by the culture. And within the family, death may occur without the phenomena of bereavement. Nevertheless it is clear that bereavement is typically a *family* crisis." (1 p. 184)

To see what the immediate effects of a death are in the home let us look at it before and after death strikes. Normally members of the family develop an adjustment of responsibilities among themselves— as well as an equilibrium of relations between each other in the matters affecting the home, especially the status and the roles of each. They learn how to get along with each other, and set up a pattern of habitual individual and joint activities. Emotional security for each one is dependent on the continuance of the scheme of mutual relations that has been established. Expectations of future welfare for each are related closely to continuity of family ties or planned changes in them. In the normal home many of the deepest affections are associated with the complementary roles of the mother, father, sons and daughters.

It is this organization that is broken by the death of any one of the family. With the break up of the pattern of familiar give and take, feelings of insecurity and uncertainty may possess one or all of its members. The disorganizing effect of death becomes more pronounced with lack of preparation for its occurrence. From this summary analysis of the disrupting results of death on the family, and the difference between it and the effect on the wider circle of acquaintances, two deductions of importance in the conduct of the funeral can be made. The first has to do with the divergence between the emotional needs at a funeral of those persons who are experiencing bereavement and those who are not.

There is a common assumption that one tone, grief, sounds throughout the entire cycle of gatherings held to pay respects to a departed associate. In an earlier period of history, the distinction between the sorrow of the family and that of friends and neighbors did not hold so clearly. Despite the fact that the family was a more cohesive group, it was not so distinct from the community as it is now. The community, in the sense of social relations, was more compact too. Death in a small integrated group was a serious deprivation for the whole community; the funeral solemnized common deprivation. When communities grew larger and the vital matters of social import were affected but slightly by a single death, a fiction of great sorrow dominating the funeral persisted.

The fiction of community sorrow remained, partly at least, because it served to sharpen the dramatic appeal of the ceremony. The symbols of death are survivals from the past, and are therefore largely reminders of dejection and distress. In a time when family and community were tied together closely they were appropriate for the series of funeral developments in larger measure than at present. The change in the proportionate size of the family group has also detracted from the dominance of the feelings of its members at the more inclusive assemblages after death has occurred. Families, three generations ago, formed in each case a larger fraction of the total community group. The family, too, was of greater importance then than now among the institutions of the community. In these and other ways the feelings of the entire group at a funeral resembled the grief of the family.

Irrelevance of Outward Proceedings to Bereavement. The second deduction to be drawn from an understanding of the nature of bereavement has bearing on a fiction promulgated by funeral directors, namely, that grief of the sorrowing family and close friends is assuaged by the elegance of the casket, and the funeral parlor and by the use of ultra-modern equipment. It is true that at the period in which the funeral is held insights may come to the bereaved persons that will have enduring effects. But that the external aspects of a funeral have any but the most superficial relation to deep sorrow is a groundless assumption.

In addition to the testimony of many persons, there are three logical factors showing the high degree of improbability of a causal connection. First, funerals are uniform in pattern within a given culture and economic group. On the other hand the reaction of individuals to the loss of close associates is characterized most conspicuously by its variability, depending on a number of factors, particularly the personality pattern of the mourner.

Individuals in different social categories also react diversely to the loss of intimate associates. Landis finds that men left alone after years of marriage are more helpless than widows, a fact which probably accounts for their remarrying in greater numbers than women. Widows in the age group of twenty to forty-five may face an unfortunate lot, since small children are apt to be left with the surviving wife, complicating their family adjustment with the problem of family support. (2, p. 292) Between the bereavement of the widow and the unmarried woman there are these distinctions, as reported by Dickinson and Beam: "The widow suffers under severe sexual tension in an intense reliving of the marriage. While 'the single woman's conflict is with imagination; the married woman's conflict is with reality.'" (3, p. 270)

Old age, too, conditions reaction to bereavement: "Probably the most important single factor determining whether one shall cease to mourn after a reasonable time is age. The old have great difficulty in giving up their libidinal attachments and cannot easily make a new start." (4, p. 506)

There is nothing to be found to indicate that funerals reflect the variability among bereaved persons in the matter of personality patterns of the mourners.

A second characteristic in which there is great discrepancy between the nature of bereavement and the funeral is the length of time taken up by each. The whole series of events connected with a funeral takes from one to six or seven days, three or four days being standard. A glance at the statements of students of bereavement quickly reveals that the stages of that experience cover months or years.

Eliot lists as typical, primary (i.e., immediate) effects of bereavement: abandon, rejection of the facts, detached calm, shock in the neurological sense, exaltation, self-injury, repression, blame of self or others, the intense longing of grief. (1, p. 185) In *Family Crises and Ways of Meeting Them,* he describes the ensuing struggle between acceptance and rejection of reality as taking place in long periods of uncontrolled abandon, weeping, cursing, self-blame, even self-injury. (5, p. 238)

The gradual emancipation from dependence on the loved one and adjustment to life without him involves slow emotional developments. Waller found confirmation of the conclusion of Freud that in the bereavement dream the most remarkable compromises are made between the desire to have the dead person alive again and the knowledge that he is in fact irretrievably dead. "Mourning is the process," says Waller, "in which the habits and emotions are adjusted to this verdict of reality." (4, p. 50) It is a slow and painful process.

At the conclusion of the struggle to readjust, the individual resumes normal activities in a new life pattern. He will, if successful, achieve stability in his way of living, and establish relations of satisfying give and take with other objects of attention and affection, or with persons of his old pattern on a new basis. The process is gradual, in fact may never be entirely finished. Says Eliot: "One may never feel a decision to take up life again; it is, in a sense life which takes one up again."

A third characteristic of the funeral is quite at variance with the feature of bereavement which it is expressly intended to serve—namely, the viewing of the face of the dead person. A universal contention of funeral directors is that the last look at the "restored" face of the deceased creates an image that remains permanently in the memory of the bereaved person. The burden of the claim is that the "restorative" operation of the undertaker is of great and lasting value in bereavement and the adjustive process. No evidence that this claim is justified is to be found in the works of the psychologists. However, evidence to the contrary is ascertainable, to the effect that the lasting image (the "memory image" of the funeral directors) does not usually originate in the last look at the body of the deceased but in experiences prior to that time. I quote Waller in reporting one aspect of the responses to questions he addressed to bereaved persons:

"One comes to think of the dead not as he was or as he would have wished to be, but as one would have wished him to be. As these memory flashes are released, some of the emotions connected with the bereavement are released also and the feelings are expressed in intense spasms of grief. As these feelings come out, there appears to be a powerful impulse to share the fate of the departed. . . . In the mingling of imagination and reality of the mourner idealization takes place and the lasting image of the loved one that emerges from the adjustment period is an 'archaic' one, i.e., representative of an age earlier than that of death." (4, p. 496)

Focus of Responsibility on the Family. Death in the home brings changes of two kinds to the family unit. The first, the disorganization of the internal adjustment, and with it the emotional concomitant of bereavement, we have just observed. The second is a sudden shift in its external relations to the community. At the moment of death the family finds itself in a changed social atmosphere. A different set of relations obtains between the family and not only the friends of the deceased, but also the community as a whole. Responsibility for the inauguration of the proprieties of the death situation suddenly falls on the family. In varying subcultures and social groupings in this country the responsibility varies, but universally the expectations of the community for the funeral period (including all the anxiety is felt by many persons when funerals for which they have states, as well as the structuring of religious rituals, start with that idea as a premise.

To illustrate the force of this pattern of expectancy: in some instances friends who had been visiting in the home just preceding the death when it was momentarily expected have felt aggrieved an hour or two later at the failure of the family to call them and tell them of the final demise. The ending of life was not regarded as an incident in a long and inevitable sequence, but the signal for the inception of a series of predetermined events. One reported incident though unusual, bears out the point in question. A funeral director had been at the home receiving instructions for the burial preparations thirty minutes before death occurred. At least one of the instructions involved expeditious activity on his part for which he was authorized to proceed, and which would not have entailed any untimely indication to friends and neighbors that the end had come. He delayed for hours, waiting, as he later explained, for a telephone call announcing the death. His conversation showed that he regarded the death itself as the cue for him to take over.

In most small communities there is no escape for the family from the necessity to carry out the pattern of funeral activities, except at the expense of offending friends and neighbors who consider the death the inevitable precursor of this chain of social and religious events. Omission of any feature of the funeral, customarily seen, brings queries and complaints. The "viewing of the remains" is one such feature, and instances of complaints are not infrequent when memorial services are held after cremation and there is no customary funeral. Particularly is this apt to be the case when the bodies of prominent persons are cremated.

Immediately after the death, a hurried period of preparation takes place at the home. If there is a physician or nurse present when death occurs, having been in something of a position of authority preceding that time, he or she may advise the family concerning arrangements for the funeral. If the individual has died at a hospital the influence of nurse or doctor is greater. Occasionally the clergyman is present at the time of death, and may or may not advise about arrangements to be made according to his policy or that of his church. The direct responsibility for the physical body passes from physician or nurse, if one or both are involved, back to the family at death or possibly immediately to the undertaker. It is to be noted that in

funeral activities) focus on the family. Legal formulations by the
after death by trained, paid persons. There is little opportunity for
those lay persons who want "to do something to help."

At the time of the death the family faces these responsibilities:
legally required papers are to be filled out, signed and filed; the body is
to be prepared for the funeral; a clergyman is to be invited to officiate
at the funeral; a cemetery plot to be secured and burial or cremation
arranged; ushers or pall bearers are to be invited to serve; neighbors,
friends and relatives are to be notified of opportunity for visiting
beginning in twenty-four or thirty-six hours, and also notified of
the time and place of the funeral itself; organizations with which the
deceased was connected are to be told of his death, and notices are
to be secured in the daily papers. It should be observed that in each
of these matters, the family authorizes and sets in motion activities
to be performed by different sets of organizational machinery. At
this point the undertaker comes in. He "undertakes" to get some or
all of these items arranged for properly and to see that they are all
carried out and regulated to meet time requirements.

It is in varying degrees that families turn over to funeral directors
the responsibilities of arranging items. The filing of the required
papers is specifically a duty of a funeral director or medical school
representative, and cannot be done by a member of the family. Preparation of the body is almost invariably done under the undertaker's
direction. There is at least one religious organization in the Middle
West in which the body is prepared entirely by friends, relatives and
members of the society, but legal restrictions prevent like measures
in other states. Preparation of the body is unnecessary, and may be
omitted entirely at the discretion of the family, when immediate burial
or cremation is decided upon. Transportation to the crematory in
most states must be carried out by a funeral director. Preparation
of the body is not arranged for when the body is to be turned over
to a medical school.

Whatever may be the measure in which it delegates its responsibility
to the undertaker, the family remains the central figure in the meetings that follow. Since its members are the principal actors, they
take a unique role in the funeral gatherings. They are in that sense
different from the others and in greater or less degree set apart. To
the extent they feel the pressure of propriety, their greatest desire is
to have the arrangements and the procedures in accordance with approved usage. Ritual and anxiety are said to go together. Certainly

these cases the body is ministered to, sometimes both before and made arrangements are taking place.

The Sense of Guilt. The two effects of a death upon the immediate home associates, namely grief and disorganization of the established pattern of mutual reactions, and the sudden emergence of these individuals into the focus of responsibility for group proceedings—these two, operating simultaneously, almost without exception, create a sense of guilt in the responsible persons. This feeling is not always recognized as such by those who experience it. It is seldom spoken of freely, since it is more popular to speak only of grief on the occasion. Actually, however, guilt is almost an inevitable accompaniment of grief and anxiety at funerals. This sense of guilt is not necessarily associated with any memory of having harmed the deceased. It is a feeling that results from several factors and enters the consciousness of the individual because of the situation he is in.

First, it would seem, there is a projection of the sorrow that is felt onto the person who is dead. He is pitied, although it is obvious that he is not suffering. The sorrow that is projected is not alone regret for the loss of a companion, but partly (perhaps largely) a renewed realization that each must die, and hence sorrow for oneself. In the play, *The Dragon's Mouth,* by Jacquetta Hawkes and J. B. Priestley, something of the same idea is illustrated. The four passengers who criticize one another harshly and admire themselves excessively, learn that one of them, they do not know which, will be dead in a day or two. They thereupon change completely the burden of their conversation, each speaking generously of the others and ruthlessly dealing with himself.

Second, the bereaved person is in the center of attention of a large number of his acquaintances, and is expected to show affection for the one he has lost through death. Under such circumstances a strong impulse to belittle self and praise the dead would be normal.

A third factor must operate in many cases, if not all. Aversion to the dead body is felt at a time when the survivor has been made tragically aware of affection for the dead person. Reaction to any consciousness of the aversion at that juncture must take the form of guilt. It is from the combination of the component emotions that a persistent sense of guilt arises. In any case, whether or not the analysis given is accurate, observation makes it abundantly clear that guilt is the predominating emotion under the circumstances. It becomes a very potent influence on the principal actors in funeral situations. It is not by any means always a positive and rational force.

CHAPTER III

GROUP BEHAVIOR AT FUNERAL GATHERINGS

That short, potential stir
That each can make but once,
That bustle so illustrious
'Tis almost consequence,
Is the *éclat* of death.
                              EMILY DICKINSON

The arrangements the family makes for a funeral provide typically for three, sometimes four, types of gatherings. At all of them, except the fourth, the casket containing the remains is observed by all in attendance. These are: the wake, the religious ceremony, the committal service at which the casket is lowered into the grave, and possibly the gathering at the home after the more formal and public sessions are over. The reasons for holding several instead of one long observance are the necessity to hold the differing stages of the funeral in the rooms of suitable size, style, and equipment; the prohibitive length of time that would be required if one meeting only were held; the need to offer alternative days or hours to accommodate persons with crowded calendars; the desirability of providing separate occasions in order that groups of differing composition may attend differing types of assemblages; and lastly, the danger of blurring the impression made at any one of the occasions if it were associated too closely with the others. The gatherings vary greatly, not only in composition and affective tone, but in type of activity indulged in, in solidarity of the groups, and in leadership.

The Sociable Wake. The wake is a period during which the embalmed body lies in the casket to be looked at by visitors. It is also designated as "lying in state." The first term originated in a custom, rarely still practiced, of relatives sitting up all night with the body. The second term, "lying in state," applied originally to the bodies of notables, as they lay on exhibition for the benefit of followers. Neither term is descriptive as applied generally today. The expressed reason for attending is to pay respects to the dead, or to offer sympathy to the close relatives who are always present. However, the "viewing of the body" and the expression of sympathy are only the traditional and the proper performances expected of visitors. In the majority of cases they are briefly and sometimes perfunctorily accomplished. Attention then reverts, if the visitors remain for any length of time, to friendly and casual conversation with the others present. It takes up the greater part of the time usually spent at the wake.

In approximately six out of ten cases the visiting is done at the funeral parlor, in practically all other cases at the home. (1, p. 9). Visiting usually takes place in the afternoon or evening from one to four days preceding the day of the funeral service. For most groups in the east, middle west, and south, attendance during this period is large. In the region west of the Rocky Mountains bodies lie in state for but one evening before the service. Almost universally the place in which the wake is held is made as homelike and as cheerful as possible. A few touches in the décor, especially in the vicinity of the casket, indicate the presence of death, such as two pillar-like lamps and two candles encased in colored glass. In the funeral homes pictures of a religious import, such as *The Last Supper*, are often displayed.

The most striking note in the surroundings of the casket is the large number of flowers arranged in bunches or woven into floral designs. Often they are so numerous that little or no aesthetic effect is produced. The tone of funeral parlors varies from the dreary, through the garish to the elegant. Frequently the parlors are over-elaborate. The chapels in a large establishment may each be done in a period style, or according to a dominant pattern and called "The Blue Room," "The Victorian Room," etc.

The casket containing the body is sometimes placed in the dominating spot in the room or suite of rooms. Or it may be in a niche or in a room adjoining that in which the visitors congregate. Sometimes the casket can not easily be seen from the seats or standing places of the majority of persons in the group. Clergymen or representatives of groups who come to say prayers only, or to hold a service, may stand near the casket. Sermons or talks, however, will be delivered often from a speaker's vantage point without reference to the situation of the body. The visitors who do more than make an appearance, look at the deceased and speak to a member of the family, distribute themselves in the most available spots and in formations which are most favorable for group conversation and discussion.

Typically the wake is held for the whole world of acquaintances and connections of the person who has died. It is the occasion, while he lies in state, for each individual who knew him to see him for the last time, personally to offer condolences to widow, mother or son, to tell of his connections with the one who is being honored, and to praise him. It is the opportunity also for representatives of the organizations to which he has belonged to bring word to his relatives and friends of the place he took in their work and companionship. That this occasion should be regarded in certain sectors of society, especially in certain cultural groups, as the biggest bid for recognition of a lifetime is not difficult to understand. Recognition comes seldom in these groups. The desire for it on the part of the members of the bereaved family is projected on to the dead person. That the thrill of the hour in the lime-light fails to stir the deceased is obvious, but it is not altogether true that anticipation of it has no effect on him. The fact can be seen in the many references in story, drama and every day life to a desire for a brilliant funeral.

The periods in which the body lies in state, especially those in the evening, provide opportunity for delegations of varying sizes to pay their respects. From the work shop, store, society or church come associates, or a group officially representing the job, section, committee or project. Status is one determining factor in the selection of the personnel of delegations. Frequently the job boss, or any other immediate superior comes and gives a tone of added importance to the occasion. In small communities those in attendance represent all walks of life. The strongest selective factor is church affiliation. In large communities economic status is the greatest determining factor in the composition of the attendance at the wake. Ethnic origin plays a powerful part, especially as it is associated with religious differences. This holds for national origin among minority groups, especially in the first and second generations. The ownership of the funeral parlor selected by the family corresponds usually to the race, creed and national origin of the family of the deceased, in response to common loyalties and because of greater understanding of group habits in the social activities of the wake.

In the gatherings of the wake the influence of the church is exercised in varying degrees, but, with the exception of Pentecostal groups, less than at the ceremony and the committal service. However, church groups in any denomination may appear at the wake in numbers or by representative delegations. Often in evangelical circles the minister, his assistant, or lay leaders of the church conduct short religious sessions such as prayers, Scripture readings, or songs. In groups of greatest church solidarity a sermon may be given on one of the evenings. At wakes in Catholic groups a priest often appears to say a prayer. Some Protestant ministers refrain from attendance, feeling that the wake is purely social, and that it is best for them to wait for the serious note that will be sounded at the church service. The most formal incidents at some wakes are the services conducted by certain of the fraternal orders. Veterans groups offer formal services to be held at the wake, or military honors to be performed at the grave. There are wakes at which as many as five fraternal services have been given, although some of the larger orders provide their ceremony on condition it is the only one to be held.

Activity at the wake is predominantly social intercourse. When a large number of persons is present, as is often true in the evening, the occasion becomes a party. Some groups are more reverential or subdued than others. Some wear ordinary clothing; some "dress up." They talk about their usual interests, as well as those of the deceased. Most of them speak about the likeness to life of the face of the dead acquaintance. Some of them seem consciously to avoid mention of the body.

As in all social matters there are examples of extremes of behavior: In the Pentecostal groups revelrous lamentation is prolonged. There are degrees of conviviality to be found in different groups. Joking at the wake is practiced in more than one cultural group. The assertion that joking is more cruel than sober expression of sympathy to members of the family is not borne out by inquiry. In fact many persons defend joking as less cruel. They say they make an effort "to say silly things about ourselves and the deceased" and thus to take the minds of the bereaved family off the grievous aspects of their loss, to "tide them over the worst period." I have been unable, through many queries, to find anyone accustomed to the practice who has felt hurt by it.   (2, pp. 168-9)

Ribaldry at wakes is also a matter of degree, governed by the prevailing convivial habits of the group in question. Funeral directors report that men, especially those of certain cultural groups want to bring in food and drinks. Few establishments allow either. However one funeral home known to the author has a cafeteria on the premises. Members of the lower income groups sometimes bring soft drinks into the funeral chapels.

There are two main factors in the reduction of the hilarious aspects of the wake: (1) the more public atmosphere of the funeral parlor as

compared to the home, and (2) the rules laid down by funeral directors, setting a closing hour at 9, 10, or 11 o'clock, or discouraging visiting hours after a given time. The elegance of many funeral establishments has added to the suppression of hilarity on the part of
many groups.

One striking characteristic of wakes is the comparative lack of
leadership in most of them. No one "starts anything" beyond the
possible ushering into the proper room by an attendant at the funeral
parlor, and beyond the first formality of looking at the face of the
deceased and speaking to the chief mourners. The words of a visiting
delegation, the prayer of a clergyman, or the service of a fraternal
organization may constitute a formal ritual. On the whole, however,
the discussion is informal, carried on in small casual groups.

Though emotions experienced at the wake are many and varied, it
is the least emotional meeting of the series of funeral assemblages.
The chief mourners usually express their gratitude for the many statements of sympathy. A large attendance swells their pride. For
some families, the numerous floral pieces, the glamour of the casket,
or even the mere knowledge of the costliness of the arrangements, creates a sense of prestige. The most universal wish is "to do the right
thing" for the dead one. The right thing is to accord him recognition by providing for the occasion an aura of splendor. The number
and importance of those in attendance magnify the sense of prestige.

For the members of the family the wake may be fatiguing, lasting,
as it often does, for many hours. Often the prolonged experience is
an ordeal. Little time is left the family for the routine tasks, and
the consequent pressure creates tension that mounts until the day of
the funeral. The funeral parlor provides for some of the satisfaction of entertaining in a spacious room, for others, however, the
strangeness of its surroundings is depressing. For a very considerable number the place and the proceedings seem pretentious, out of
keeping with their feelings about the mystery of life and death. The
terms they use to describe the sessions of the wake include "superficial,"
"barbarous," "pagan." For them the lavish display is wasteful in the
highest degree. Many feel revulsion at the public aspect of the wake,
especially the submission of the "restored" face of the dead to the
curious or morbid gaze of all who come. Some complain that the
atmosphere is not that of home or church, but is charged with commercialism, at a time when commercialism should have no place.

In small towns and in isolated groups the wake is often a moving experience. In larger towns, especially when a group of greater size gathers, it is likely to become a casual matter. For the prominent citizen it becomes a public affair, devoted largely to viewing the body; for the unknown pauper it is dispensed with.

The Ritual Service. The funeral service is the third stage of the funeral proceedings, following the preparations in the home, and the wake. It is different from the wake in almost all particulars. For one thing it is a brief ceremony as compared with the sessions of the preceding stage. It is formal in content and procedure, in the church setting in which it is held, and even in the attire of those attending. At the wake, friends and relatives are inclined to lighten the spirit of the occasion and often to avoid the mournful aspects of the death; at the funeral service the most serious of death's meanings are confronted. Except in very rare instances the service is intended to be a serious and sobering experience. (2, pp. 317-339)

The funeral service is a ritual lying traditionally in the province of the church. Even among non church members, the majority of persons look upon the church as the place for the holding of the service, or on a clergyman, bringing the message of the church to the funeral parlor, as the appropriate individual to officiate. There are exceptions, as in the case of brief ceremonies of the family and friends at home or in funeral parlors, in which there is no clerical leadership but rather that of the elder member, friend, or organization official. The relation of the funeral to the essential activities of the church varies among denominations and among churches within one denomination. In some instances it is strictly a church affair and the members are all expected to put in an appearance. In others, it may be peripheral in its relation to the congregational aspect of the church, or regarded as a matter of chief concern only to the clergyman and the bereaved family.

On the whole, fewer persons attend the church service than come at one time or another to the wake. In metropolitan areas the funeral service of a prominent leader in a minority group is often the occasion for a mass demonstration of solidarity that fills the largest church and throngs the street on which it stands.

At the service emphasis is put on the seating arrangements for the participants and on the sequence of events. The casket is placed in front of the group, with the closest relatives nearest to it, and those of less connection with the deceased further back. In the church the clergyman is in the most prominent position at the altar or in the pulpit; the pall bearers and any other dignataries of the occasion are also near the front. When the service is over the same relative status of positions is maintained in the procession to the cemetery. Events in the ritual take place in automatic sequence rather than by verbal direction of a leader. At services in mortuary homes the sequence is less fixed and the undertaker, who assumes very little prominence at a church, directs affairs more actively in his own premises.

At the wake much verbal interaction takes place. At the service practically none occurs; the audience is silent except as it may take part in responses led by the clergyman. In fact the clergyman initiates all action, except that directed by the funeral director. Activity on the part of the auditors is of an unexpressed emotional or intellectual kind.

When a eulogy is given, the keenest attention of the members of the audience is devoted to identification of each with the dead person. After the funeral, they tell of listening for items in the narration of the life or in the characterization of the eulogy with which they were familiar, or events or loyalties which they shared with the deceased. The desire to listen to a eulogy rather than to an analysis and critical evaluation of the life that is ended, comes in part from this identification, and the consequent egoistic satisfaction in praise and commendation that directly or remotely reflects on them.

However, a much stronger emotion creates or strengthens the wish to hear well of the dead. It is the wish to be well spoken at ones own funeral. Under the weight of the apprehension, whether clearly or vaguely realized as such, the individual gains some assurance through hearing words of approbation. In this connection one emotional experience at the funeral service needs to be mentioned here. It will be dealt with more fully from another approach in Chapter XII. This experience is the concern that is usually aroused over the mystery of life and death and the often painful reappraisal of the ideals held by the individual and the degree to which they are implemented in the routine of daily affairs. Clergymen occasionally find persons ready to affiliate or renew affiliation with the church when death has occurred in the family.

Due to the depth of feeling aroused by death in the minds of some of those in attendance, and due also to the grief of the close friends and relatives, there is always the possibility of an outburst of emotional expression, especially in the case of a few minority groups. The clergy, for the most part, take precautions to prevent the occurrence, some meet with the members of the family before the ceremony to fortify them against the emotional ordeal. Tensions of other kinds are experienced during the ceremony by some of the members of the congregation; sympathy with the bereaved, remembrance of similar losses in the past, fear or expectation of an emotional outburst, or, among those present who are not adherents of the faith expressed in the ritual, an uneasiness at participation in it.

In a gathering of any considerable size, there are also persons who are emotionally affected very little. Many persons who are deeply affected are fatigued by the contemplation of death. To meet these tensions and this fatigue clergymen reduce the service to thirty minutes or less in length. Clergymen called to officiate at a service in a funeral home, may speak voluntarily or by request for only ten minutes.

One other almost universal characteristic of funerals is the lavish display of expenditures noticeable in the costly casket. This is particularly striking at the obsequies held for the dead of low or middle income families. At services held in the chapels of undertaking establishments, the impression of conspicuous display is augmented by the mass of costly floral pieces. A real or imagined need may be served by the seemingly extravagant exhibit. Nevertheless the uninitiated observer cannot but be struck by the contrast of the social and spiritual emotions aroused by the death and emotions characterized by the superficial desire to live up to the Joneses.

A lasting impression of differences between funeral services is left by the contrasting atmosphere in which they may be held. In the home of the deceased a tone of familiarity with him and his "folks" prevails. Sympathy for the family is felt more intensely than in either of the other two settings, and simplicity of casket and procedure seems eminently appropriate. The participant's mind is apt to dwell on the family life of the deceased, its beginning and its now partial dissolution, as well as on the generation immediately preceding and the one following his. At the church the symbols of faith make their imprint, and solemnity as well as architectural grandeur seem fitting. Here not only the deceased and his family, but the gathering itself becomes merely a part of the expression of ultimate human longings. The mind of the participant in this context dwells less on the period of a lifetime and more on vast stretches of time and on the meaning of eternity. In a sense the funeral parlor is more informal than either the home or church. It symbolizes death to the participant more than they, and in greater measure holds the attention to this one unusual happening. It magnifies the present anguish and guilt and glosses over the permanence of affection and sorrow, and the continuing processes of daily living. It emphasizes, not so much the span of life nor the long stretch of time, but the short period of the funeral activities.

Finality of the Committal Service. Committing the remains to the earth is a continuation of the funeral service. It is dramatic beyond any incident in the funeral period except the moment of death itself. It is packed with acts and symbols of finality, and if ritual could blot out any lingering fantasy that the dead one might be seen or heard again, the committal would do so.

Fewer persons attend the committal service, partly because of the distressing nature of the experience there, partly because to do so is time consuming. This is particularly true in urban centers where the cemetery lies at a considerable distance from residential areas. In addition, many acquaintances entertain the opinion that the final act affects specifically only the closest relations and friends. On occasion, when the clergyman has been brought in to officiate at the service of a stranger, or when the journey to the grave is long, the committal service is said incongruously in the funeral parlor before the procession starts. Thereafter few but the immediate family accompany the casket. If the deceased has been prominent, or a member of a cohesive group, larger numbers of persons make the trip. It is still quite a common thing for the surviving members of the family to take pride in the number of cars in the procession.

During the last and climactic episode of the funeral series the casket is the center of attention. Lines of status are drawn as at the preceding service. The hearse leads the procession, followed by the immediate family, other relatives, near friends and others in order. The clergyman and pall bearers ride in cars near the head of the cortege. At the end of the journey the clergyman and the immediate relatives stand closest to the grave. The undertaker becomes much more prominent in the direction of the proceedings as he and his assistant instruct the pall bearers in placing the casket on the tapes and later lowering it into the grave.

The rite is brief; the trend is to make it less harrowing for those who have lived with the one who now is dead. But feelings run deep and strong and are more likely to burst out here than at any other time. Often the clergyman bolsters the closest relatives before the committal begins. As the casket is lowered and the symbolic flowers or handful of earth is thrown on the casket and particularly when the phrase "dust to dust" is heard, the tension is almost unbearable for any one who has known the deceased at all well, but especially for the family. At this moment, in certain cultural groups, a widow may attempt to throw herself on the casket and plead to go with her husband. The observer may recognize it as a role she is expected to play, and may be prepared to discount the sincerity of the act. Witnessing the enactment of just such a scene, however, leads to the firm conviction that under the cruel circumstances, the role the widow plays must be easy to assume with a maximum of tense emotion and a minimum of pretense.

The committal service might be characterized as a rite to confirm to the participants the end of their relationship to the dead, and as such it is an essential part of the celebration of death in certain religious groups. For some persons, however, it is a harrowing anti-climax to the calm sublimity of the funeral service.

The Return Home. From the moment of death, and in case of critical illness preceding it for a period before death, through the afternoons and evenings of the wake, through the tense emotional experience of the funeral service and the tragic moments of the committal service, the family has spent its physical and mental strength. The stimulus of responsibility in prominent roles has enabled the members to hold out to the end. When the cultural requirements have been met and the spotlight removed, the return to the home may signalize a let-down into more heart rending sorrow than any happening up to that time. The old relationships have been disrupted, and the new not yet entered upon. It is then that some of the neighbors or the relatives not included in the immediate family often try to make the home-coming seem less lonesome and desolate. They prepare food, either in the home of the family or in their own homes, and bring it in for the tired and hungry group. Such assistance has become a custom that is to be found in many parts of the country.

Usually few persons are present, unless many relatives have come from outside the city to remain for a gathering of the extended family. Action originates with the neighbors, relatives and close friends; and ordinarily, as in any housekeeping matter, the women take over the planning and serving of food. There is little or no formality, and a warm, intimate feeling pervades the group.

The impulse of the close associates to lessen the work and brighten the spirit of the return home does not arise solely from a rational consideration of the need of the family. It springs from a desire of practically every one who has known the family in a friendly fashion. From the hour when death is expected or has come many offer help, and many more would do so if they could think of some service that is needed.

It would appear first that some glimmering of the pressure of formal requirements of the funeral on the family is felt. Second the sympathy that is felt finds verbal expression difficult for many persons and inadequate for many more. Occasionally the observer detects something of the feeling of guilt that the chief mourners experience also gripping in smaller measure the less intimate friends and neighbors. The wish "to do something" is its manifestation.

PART II

THE FUNERAL BUSINESS

CHAPTER IV

"BEHIND THE SCENES"

Death, the stern sculptor, with a touch
No earthly power can stay,
Changes to marble in an hour
The beautiful, pale clay.
LOUISA MAY ALCOTT

In Part I the aim is to describe the happenings at the funeral, somewhat in the sequence in which they occur. As part of the description, the situations in which the happenings took place have been
sketched as a background, and so far as has been possible, the emotional accompaniments of the actions have been reported. Here a
different point of view is taken. An effort is made to get behind the
scenes depicted in Part I in order to get at the causes for the happenings previously described. Each chapter will relate what takes place
in a typical funeral, such as the words and actions of family and
undertaker making the arrangements, the relation of clergy and funeral directors, and the interplay between the undertaker and the
community in which he lives.

In each chapter a scene will be depicted back stage as it were, in a
spot from which the actors step on to the stage where funeral proceedings take place. Backstage each spot holds a group or set of
persons with limited interests and specific purposes to be served in
the main performance. In that performance the diverse small groups
all come together in the guise of one or more actors following out the
directions reached separately backstage.

The actions and pressures of each separate party are the result of
economic or social forces peculiar to it. In the last analysis, therefore, the effect of conditions in the total society can be seen as it

determines the motivations of each party to the funeral, and through the interplay of the parties, the happenings at that ceremony. In order to make the descriptions pertinent to the purpose in hand the parties to the funeral will be represented in action or preparing for action. The typical customer and the funeral director as individuals will be shown bargaining. So far as there is such a thing, a typical individual, shown in a typical situation, will be described in each case. In sum, Part II is intended to answer the question, "Why?" as raised by the occurrences described in Part I.

There are forces which operate on a state-wide, a regional or a national scale that help to shape the funeral. They are to be considered in their broad scope in the last chapter of this section. However the context in which the persons and groups affecting, and affected by the funeral relate to each other, is the community. For the most part the pressures on the individuals derive from customs, standards, sympathies and loyalties which operate in the community. To get the sense of interrelatedness within the community I have used the undertaker as the focal figure, observing him in his relations to the typical persons with whom he deals. The responsiveness of the undertaker to the influence of the customer, the minister, the priest or rabbi, the social worker, or the representatives of other community interests, is a part of this phase of the study.

CHAPTER V

THE BARGAINING SITUATION:
FAMILY AND UNDERTAKER

And all the gold from here to Babylon might burn
To dross, unminded, for we bore our dead.
GEORGE ALLAN ENGLAND

Unique among buyer-seller relationships is that between the funeral director and his customer. Into it the representative of the family enters with unusual motivations and under abnormal pressures. The undertaker, too, in his relations with the family of the deceased, plays a role in his own eyes unlike that of any other seller. In addition, the rules of the game are not comparable to the generally accepted regulations governing buying and selling.

The responsibilities of each party to the transaction determine in part the nature and extent of the negotiations. The member of the family who makes the arrangements for the funeral finds himself responsible to see that certain details are carried out. He is called upon to see that all sanitary regulations are complied with; that the body is not kept without treatment for more than a brief period; that official records are made of the death; and that all other bureaucratic formalities are attended to. Second, traditionally he is looked to by friends and neighbors to initiate, carry through, and pay for, the responsibilities mentioned above, and for a culturally determined series of events that make up the funeral assemblages. He is under even more critical scrutiny by relatives from far and near, to see that the status of the family is upheld and that the social connections of the deceased are ended with propriety or preserved in some measure for the family.

The funeral director is responsible, first, for seeing to it that materials are purchased and helpers engaged to carry out the wishes of the family in regard to the burial. Once he has been commissioned by the family it is his responsibility to see that ordinances and laws regarding disposal of deceased persons are observed, and to see that any evidence of criminal acts in bringing about the death is revealed to the proper authorities. He is expected to carry out the wishes of the family with respect to the religious or other cultural patterns of procedure, to fit into the demands of church, lodge or other officiating body, and to carry out the details of arrangements according to instructions of the family. In those matters in which laws or ordinances have defined his role the funeral director is obligated to carry through duties without client approval. In other matters he is not only engaged as an agent, but subject in detail to the approval or disapproval of the family or its representative. The job is not turned over to him as a patient turns direction of his physical care over to a physician. Distinct limits may be placed on his initiative and control by the customer.

Predispositions of Each Party. Another feature of the situation in which customer and funeral director meet is the predispositions in the minds of each. They come together with expectations often never expressed, often in fact, beneath consciousness. The less aware either may be of the presence of these patterns of expectation in his own subconscious mind, the more difficult it becomes for him to deal rationally on the points in question. The undertaker has an impulse to urge a "nice" funeral, for reasons other than personal profit. Because of his personal identification with it he feels a sense of belittlement if his standards of excellence are not met. Often, he has been given great freedom in the determination of many features. He is sure he knows better than the purchaser what should be done. He has had the satisfaction of taking care with finality of certain items in the total program of previous funerals. The result is a distinct tendency to tell clients what they should do, or what "is being done," or to attempt to interpret what outward forms the sentiments of the bereaved should assume at the funeral, such as the provisions of costly floral pieces. The universal picture in the mind, or at any rate in the words, of the funeral director, is that the funeral, in which he is engaged come up to the current standard of excellence of the business.

There are numerous complaints by funeral directors about their customers. They help to reveal their predispositions in entering upon negotiations. One leader in the vocation cited as a prototype of all complaints the hotel guest who wants coffee brewed in his room. "He upsets the intricate operation of the hotel." The undertaker is impatient of any extraordinary request. He has a pattern of procedure from which he dislikes to deviate. He complains about the mere fact of criticism, not necessarily its extent or unreasonableness; he feels chagrin that the coiffure was not appreciated; and he resents the propensity of a few clients to complain. A prominent leader of funeral directors writes: "Unusual requests of clients are generally the most difficult to serve. People who do unconventional things create problems."

The funeral director enters the negotiations with his client in the hope that the client will be persuaded to accept what he, the funeral director, customarily has to offer. His establishment is geared to offer one of a number of designs of funerals. Clients of the working class accept those designs with greatest satisfaction; wealthy patrons pay for any deviations. Individuals in the professional and artistic group are the ones who complain most and who are resented because of their tendencies to want to model their funerals upon the pattern of their own group culture or their own idiosyncracies. Further complicating the bargaining situation for the undertaker, and usually masked to himself as well as his customer, is whatever reservoir of resentment he has stored up because of slights he has felt, due to the nature of his business.

A predisposition that further complicates the bargaining situation is an aversion to the undertaker on the part of the customer. The aversion is increased by the uncomfortable speculation as to what will happen to the body of the one who has died. The undertakers realize that there is this concern in the minds of the customers. They reveal their comprehension by their urgings that the customers purchase strong caskets and vaults to ensure permanent preservation of the remains. They reveal their comprehension also by their efforts to dissuade customers from resort to cremation because of alleged movements of the body in the process. Inviolability of the body is, in some states assured by law, guaranteed in prospectuses of funeral service, and promised verbally by the mortician. The frequency of assurance to the customer on this point alone would be strong evidence of the trepidation. Undertakers vary widely in respect to their possession of self assurance, but there is no question but that a defensive attitude is present with many before they meet the family to negotiate the funeral. The same generalization can be made of the customers: some have no later consciousness of trepidation when making arrangements with the funeral director, but there is also, apparently, a much larger number of those who do.

Grief, because of the death, is another element affecting the attitudes of the customer during negotiations with the undertaker, and it is a powerful factor making the client vulnerable in instances. Because of it some cases of gross exploitation surely do occur. I quote a statement about the effect of grief on the client typical of the belief of several of the most outspoken and often printed critics of the funeral director—a statement true in a lamentably large number of cases: "Ordinary business motives are almost wholly lacking. The sorrowing family, in a highly emotional state, with minds dulled by grief to the reality of the funeral bill, deals with a cool-headed business man who must make his living and meet the tremendous overhead of his establishment from the sales of merchandise and his services." (1, p. 1391)

Grief on the part of the family is recognized by undertakers as a disabling factor, but the number of cases in which it leads them to moderation in recommendations for elaborate funerals seems to be very small. For the majority of them the vulnerability of the family due to grief is an advantage in the bargaining situation not to be neglected. Further, through their process of rationalization, the very grief of the family comes to be a reason for more expensive and elaborate funerals, on the assumption that the larger the expenditure the greater the solace for the grieving.

A successful funeral director made a revealing statement illustrative of one of the practitioner's possible reactions to the disabling effect of grief on the client. This statement was made in all seriousness: "The family doesn't hire a funeral director to weep with it; it hires and wants a normal mind to guide and advise its abnormal minds in every manner, financial and otherwise, that it may show proper respect to its deceased according to customs and caste. For the want of a better expression, let me say that the new funeral director is working on the professional side as a Doctor of Grief, or expert in returning abnormal minds to normal in the shortest possible time, and on the business side toward becoming a trained and skilled business executive." (2, p. 27)

From a large number of families interviewed there comes not the slightest evidence that they hired an undertaker to guide their "abnormal minds." They have all declared that they were ready to make their decisions, but desired to do so in the light of facts and under no pressure. Many resent any attempt to influence them.

It has been pointed out by some of the most objective leaders among the funeral directors that grief seldom disorganizes a person to the extent assumed by the writer above, or, for that matter, by the severest critics of the undertaker. Further, the arrangements for a funeral are not infrequently turned over to a representative of the family whose control of himself is not seriously impaired. Still further, grief sometimes results in increased suspicion and a drive by the client toward hard bargaining demands. It is quite safe to say, however, that grief operates in a majority of cases to take funeral negotiations out of the realm of normal bargaining operations, and renders the families vulnerable to pressures brought upon them. It is also surely true that they face the funeral director alone, without support in an unusual and painful situation.

The most powerful as well as the most universal force playing on the family at the time it meets the funeral director is the sense of guilt. In the negotiations it is seldom, if ever, referred to, and is undoubtedly unrecognized at the time as guilt. It is the inner drive, however, which responds most compulsively when the undertaker accuses the clients, by word or implication, of little love for the dead if the funeral falls short of the most expensive outlay the family can scrape together. One illustration is typical of many instances. A social worker and his wife tell of their self accusations when his mother died, and of their going into debt in consequence to provide a lavish funeral. Weeks later they came to the point of discussing objectively the lack of any cause for their feeling of guilt, and in this more realistic mood deplored the excessive expenditure. They have now made arrangements for simple and much less costly funerals for themselves.

Guilt felt by a surviving member of the family is sometimes a sense of shame because he fails to be grief stricken by the death, and therefore feels he is falling short of the pattern of sorrow expected of him by the community. The impulse of a person in such a situation is as strongly toward lavish display as that of one who feels deep grief. In *The Magic Mountain* Thomas Mann refers to it: "What we call mourning for our dead is perhaps not so much grief at not being able to call them back as it is grief at not being able to want to do so." The threat of death brings out tense realization and remorse for one's own shortcomings and pretensions. The bereaved person expresses the feeling of humility engendered by the death through lavish provision for the funeral of his associate. Thwarted ambition for wealth on the part of the bereaved leads him to make great expenditures for the last rite of his friend.

While guilt operates in the negotiations to render the buyer vulnerable to suggestions of extravagance, it also has an effect on the seller. The sense of guilt felt by some funeral directors is associated with their natural desire for many "cases" and the knowledge that this desire may be interpreted as a wish for the death of friends. They are aware of the numerous jokes which suggest their supposed wish that their friends and acquaintances die. A sense of guilt felt by undertakers undoubtedly would manifest itself in various ways. For the most part, however, its influence can be accounted for in the defensive attitudes to be found among them, the group rationalizations of their own importance, and the justifications they devise for the manipulation of customers.

Another of the factors that create a disposition to deal with the customer in a fashion not to be explained by the obvious developments in the negotiations, is that of anxiety or over-eagerness on the part of the funeral director. It may arise from a consciousness of his great need of customers if the business is not doing well. The over-eagerness may be present, even when the business is prosperous, due to the period of waiting that occurs between "cases" for a large fraction of undertakers. This seems to be one factor in the tendency to go to extremes in dealing with the client when one is found.

The Combined Pressures of Time and Responsibility. So much for the attitudes with which the two parties come to the bargaining process. Still other potent urges operate more clearly on a conscious level. There is a "double-squeeze" inherent in the funeral situation that becomes the factor of dominant stimulus and constraint on all parties involved in it. Undertaker-client relations are particularly influenced by it. It is the pressure on the family of limited time in which to accomplish a number of tasks, many of them outside the realm of routine, coupled with the focusing of immediate responsibility to carry out social and cultural duties. The pressure felt by the client to make arrangements quickly has two effects on his bargaining capacity. He is deprived of sufficient opportunity to seek advice from authoritative sources about the selection of the funeral director. Moreover this pressure of time prevents comparison of prices at various funeral homes. This is the factor involved in Blanshard's statement that there is no accepted, well organized "bargain counter" to which the client may go. (3, p. 682)

On the funeral director the shortage of time to accomplish the duties connected with a funeral operates differently. It adds emphasis to his tendency to develop patterns of funerals which he can pull out of stock the moment there is word from a client. His desire to tell what should be done is fortified, and any inclination to carry out unusual requests is weakened. Furthermore, he is anxious that when a death occurs his name will come to the minds of the family. His tendency to become a "joiner" of societies of all kinds is therefore strengthened. This is true particularly of the proprietor of a small or moderate establishment. The directors of large establishments are more apt to rely on continuous advertising. One of the most famous of them held that no one man could have a large enough number of organization connections, especially of the kind that would cause his name to be recalled, to provide sufficient patronage for a large establishment or for a chain of them.

The father-to-son nature of the succession in funeral home ownership and membership, to be spoken of later, is also affected by the factor of shortage of time. An established reputation or a network of acquaintances established by his father is cherished by the undertaker, since they serve to suggest his name to a family at the moment a death has occurred.

The pressure of time operates on the funeral director, occasionally inducing him to act in less than strict ethical fashion. The impelling circumstance is his need to get payment for the funeral immediately. A second circumstance, adding force to his sense of haste, resides in the legal impediment to reclaim casket or body after burial. A case in point is that of a woman who had moved and left no address. The funeral had taken place but the insurance money from which expenses were to be taken had not been received. The funeral director hunted up the insurance agent, offered him a large gratuity, and went with the agent when he visited the woman at the new address to which the insurance benefits had been forwarded. He demanded his money on the spot; got it and handed the tip to the insurance agent. In a later conversation he maintained that he had followed the only method open to him to get the money.

In other instances such methods as forcibly making a search of the house to find a check book said to be lost are cited as justified, because to fail in immediate collection is very likely to forfeit any payment. A saying that is not uncommon among undertakers when off-guard, and applied by them to persons of all economic levels, urges unconditionally to "get the money while the tears are still flowing." It is more realistic than unfeeling, in my judgment. However, it must be remembered that methods vary among types of clientele. Practices that would be understood and more or less accepted by families in one neighborhood might be highly objectionable in another.

Role of Technical Competence. An element enters into the bargaining discussions which is so common in buyer-seller relations that it is taken for granted or ignored. It consists of the technical skill and the possession by the undertaker of facilities suited to the conduct of funerals. A high degree of technical skill and the ownership of funeral facilities provide the basis for a claim by the undertaker for a free hand in the conduct of the funeral. They also serve as a basis for relatively high remuneration. What are the facts about funeral services from this standpoint? What are the claims of the undertakers; and in what light do the customers regard their services? These questions are pertinent to a further understanding of the relations between these two principal parties to the arrangements to be made.

A summary look at the items in the typical performance of the undertaker will afford a factual basis on which to form a judgment of the degree of technical or other competence involved in his role. Ordinarily he learns of the need of his services by a telephone call from the client. At that moment, only a few essential facts are asked, including the name and address of the client and the deceased, and the name of the attending physician. A trip is made immediately to the home; information is secured for the death certificate and the burial permit. The body is removed to the funeral establishment and preparations are made for embalming. (This process can be performed at the residence if requested, but requires extra work there, and involves less adequate equipment.) The physician's signature to the certificate is secured and is filed in the office of the local registrar of vital statistics.

Usually on the next day the family member, taking charge of arrangements comes to the funeral parlor, determines what casket and grave vault, if any, are to be used, and plans with the funeral director the details of the funeral, including: the days and hours the body will lie in the "reposing room"; when visitors will be welcome; what flowers, if any, are to be secured by the undertaker for the client; how many cars are to be provided for the cortege; what clergyman will be asked to officiate at the funeral or memorial service; whether the service is to be at home, at church or the funeral parlor; what pall bearers are to be asked, and by whom (undertaker or client); what music is to be provided; what cemetery is to be used, or when cremation is to occur and with what group, if any, present as the body arrives; what notices are to be placed in the papers; and what information is to be given in an obituary article. At this time the price of all services and materials is determined. The ability of the family to pay the total cost as well as the method of payment is gone into. (This matter is to be treated in a later portion of this chapter.)

A matter of first importance in any analysis of the place of the funeral director in his relations with the client, or his position in the community, is the advice he offers to the client. His advice deals frequently with amounts and channels through which the customer may secure governmental benefits, application for insurance due him, as well as a large variety of other subjects. The arrangements planned in the conference are then carried out in whole or in part by the funeral director, the client reserving such matters as he chooses for his own disposition. Typically, the body is placed in the casket and put in the reposing room which is decorated with flowers, candles or such other articles as were planned for. Frequently the funeral establishment advances money for various articles or services such as the opening of the grave. Of importance is the arrangement with the clergyman before obituary notices are sent to the papers and the recording of legally required items. Of less importance to the bargaining situation are these duties: receiving flowers and noting the senders' names, providing a door-man to receive and direct callers during the periods of the wake, furnishing a book for the names of visitors as a list for later acknowledgments.

On the day of the services the funeral director arranges the floral pieces and the chairs, directs the ushers, helps the clergyman, organizes the funeral cortege, directs the placing of the flowers in the car for it, and instructs the pall bearers in the handling of the casket. He directs the procession before or after the services in the "viewing" of the body, if that practice is followed, and closes the casket at the proper time.

At the cemetery he directs the pall bearers in the placing of the casket on the lowering apparatus in or without its vault, provides the clergyman with a trowel of earth and relatives with single flowers to cast on the casket as it is lowered, wholly or partially. He operates the lowering device, before or after the group has left, removes the equipment, grass mat, tent, or whatever materials he has brought, and starts the men filling the grave.

These are not all the details the funeral directors are prone to list when they describe their work, but those listed above indicate the nature of their duties. They are given here fully to provide a basis for a classification of his performances. Perhaps the mere listing has already led the reader to a realization that they fall in something like the following categories.

First, there are a large number of the detailed activities that would be performed by the family if no funeral director were to be engaged. Arranging flowers and chairs, noting names of senders of flowers, sending invitations, arranging for clergymen, musicians, pall bearers —all these are clearly family duties, and except as they relate to the funeral home, they are done, in whole or in part, by the family. One respondent answered the question referring to the type of work done by the undertaker by saying, he is like a caterer. It is as apt a characterization of one large class of the mortician's activities as anything could be. In this same category of the undertaker's activities should be classified: the features which are essentially household duties, but for which equipment is possessed by the establishment. Folding chairs are one example.

Second, there is a small group of responsibilities required by government in the preservation of sanitary safety, in protection against premature burial, etc., in which the funeral director performs tasks that require familiarity with formalities of which the family knows little or nothing. These entail procedural acquaintance rather than the exercise of judgment, taste, or sense of propriety. They resemble the responsibilities the undertaker assumes when he arranges for the burial plot or purchases materials from commercial firms unknown to the customer. In the jargon, "he knows his way," as the client does not, around the bureaucratic institutions and commercial firms. For this group of responsibilities at least he is not a specialist, but he is *generally* useful. In this connection it is noteworthy that funeral directors assume the status of leaders among immigrant groups much more than among peoples familiar with American institutions. It is because the importance of the undertaker is great among minority group members who do not "know their way around" and need him to turn to.

The third class of activities of the funeral director are technical, namely, the embalming and "restorative" processes. Embalming involves some knowledge principally of inorganic chemistry, anatomy, bacteriology and pathology. Restoration of facial features requires this knowledge and, in addition, a degree of "artistry." A measure of the extent of technical training required for the vocation is to be found in the brevity of the period covered in attendance at schools of mortuary science, namely, nine months or one year.

There is possibly a fourth category of activities of varied nature, and slight frequency. They consist of services to the whole community, the most common of which is the provision of an ambulance for the use of any one needing it. A second is the lending of folding chairs for special family occasions or for churches or clubs. Here and there a firm can be found which offers to anyone in the community information about matters that have become thoroughly known to its staff, such as: routes to follow to cemeteries; the way to file a deed, etc. These services are not universally offered, and are not within the realm of the essential work of a funeral director. They are in the nature of advertising or public relations.

Funeral directors have maintained that as many as eighty man hours of service are given on an average for each funeral conducted. From the viewpoint of objective observation of the bargaining process, the embalming and "restorative" results cannot be secured except through trained and licensed personnel possessing proper facilities. Estimation of the value of the undertaker's services would be raised to the degree that these services were regarded as necessary or important. Actually they are not indispensable, since the body need not be embalmed if disposed of shortly after death. Even when the presence of the body is required in the ritual of church or synagogue, the burial can be legally and religiously accomplished without embalming. The wake is not lessened in value except for those persons to whom the custom of "viewing" is essential. It follows then that the services depending on technical training are not altogether essential, and are dispensed with in a considerable number of funerals, as will be seen in a later chapter.

The services of the nature of home responsibilities surely are not of such a level of accomplishment that extraordinarily high rates of pay for them would be expected. Lastly, the category of responsibilities described as knowing the way around government and commercial agencies requires (as has been noted) no great measure of training or judgment.

Whether the funeral director's skill and facilities justify his charging high prices for them is the question to be answered here. The answer depends on the value placed on them by the customer. The customer's value judgment, in turn, depends on what he can get for how much, and where he can turn to find more satisfactory offerings. Elementary fair play requires free choice among a variety of goods and services, and among alternative sellers. Starting with such an assumption, it will be worth while to see how the knowledge, skill and facilities of the undertaker largely determine his relation to the customer.

The funeral director is prone to take every opportunity to tell of the number of activities in which he engages in a typical funeral. He is anxious that customers and the public generally know what these activities are, holding the belief that his services will be regarded more highly if such knowledge is current. A study made for the National Funeral Directors Association of the United States shows that of twenty duties listed, only six were known to fifty per cent of the persons questioned. Ten of the twenty were known to fewer than ten per cent of the respondents. Those known by the largest numbers were: embalming, furnishing of automobiles, making cemetery arrangements, providing hearse, care of flowers, and use of funeral home. A third or more of the respondents knew that the mortician made church arrangements and took care of newspaper arrangements.

The experience of arranging for a funeral results in a larger proportion of persons who know about specific services rendered by funeral directors, as indicated by the "mentions" of these services in their answers to the questions spoken of above. The percentage of those questioned who knew about the undertaker's service in processing health department permits more than doubled. However it was only 15 per cent of all answering in the first place. The per cent of those knowing that information about social security and government allowances more than doubled with the experience of arranging a funeral, but doubled only three per cent of "mentions" of this item by those new to the experience. It is the embalming and preparing the body, making cemetery arrangements and the use of facilities, automobiles, hearse, and funeral home that loom large in the public image of the benefits for which the undertaker is paid. It is fair to assume from the figures in the study that, except for the embalming, there is little expectation on the part of customers of specific expert services when they arrange for funerals.

The study for the National Funeral Directors Association bears further witness to this conclusion. The question regarding what things were especially liked was answered, says the report as follows: "The funeral director's manner and consideration are mentioned by approximately one-third of each group (those having arranged and those who have not arranged a funeral), and his general ease and efficiency are mentioned by about the same proportion."   (4, p. 13)

A large number were interviewed in this present study about their need as they saw it when they went to morticians immediately after death had occurred.   Ninety per cent responded that they were at a loss as to the steps to take.   This is the key to the problem of the undertaker's advantage over his clients.   It is not a high degree of skill on his part, nor is it a lack of competence on the part of the members of the bereaved family, it is merely that they, through the failure of common knowledge, custom or experience, do not know what to do.   Among my inquiries was a question to the family representatives asking what item in the funeral gave them the greatest satisfaction.   There was one answer given more frequently than any other, namely "general satisfaction."   Many of the funeral directors, answering the question: "What item or items please your clients most," said they gave "general satisfaction."

That competence of the funeral director is looked on by himself as chiefly a matter of general efficiency in handling a large number of details, is shown by the replies of funeral directors as to the best mechanisms by which clients may select an establishment.   The foremost reply is "by reputation."   Others are "by past performance," "the advice of friends," "clergymen," "the size of establishment," and "the length of life of the funeral home."   No reply referred to a measure of technical competence.   Clients reply that there is no approved way to measure competence.   They choose, they say, by reputation, acquaintance with a funeral director, by advice of nurse, doctor, clergyman or friends, by the general impression gained at funerals attended, the personality of the funeral director as they saw him in action, by "little things," such as the way the deceased looked, and by advertising.

The funeral directors generally replied to my question, "What in your opinion is the greatest service you render to your clients?" with these three answers: (1) "Relieve them of responsibility," (2) "Restore the appearance of the deceased," and (3) "Give solace to the bereaved."   The families responses to me agreed that the greatest service was relieving them of responsibility.   They did not, except in a few instances, regard giving solace as a service they had received. There was wide disagreement on the value of restoration of the facial appearance of the dead.

The influence of the generality of the undertaker's duties has its effect on the bargaining relationship with his customer. Out of the lack of specificity in his own responsibilities and the variety of the duties that constitute the funeral director's service, there arise two consequences. First, his urge is reinforced to take over all matters connected with a funeral, and to find the basis of his satisfaction with the effectiveness of the funeral in the measure in which he takes over. That he sometimes goes too far in this respect is shown by the complaints about his officiousness, or his assumption of minor details of the clergyman's role. The bitterest complaints of clients relate to his making arrangements, even in rare instances of selecting the casket, without the authorization of the family. This tendency to take too much authority has often been ascribed by his critics to the undertaker's desire to arrange a costly funeral. That feature enters in often. Nevertheless, a contributing factor is his lack of a specific body of knowledge of any great importance.

The other result of the spread of duties of a funeral director over many items is his exaggerated fear of and bitter antagonism to public or cooperative ownership and management of funeral establishments. He bolsters his security by laying claim to the exclusive privilege of taking care of burials. (Another side of this same attitude will be dealt with in a later chapter devoted to an anaysis of the funeral business.)

Process of Determining Expenditure. By far the most controversial issue between the funeral trade and its critics is the question of costs. For many years it has been disputed in print and out. The popular magazines periodically produce articles citing examples of exploitation by funeral directors and the journals devoted to the practitioners reply defensively. The burden of the complaint by the critics is that funeral directors take unfair advantage of clients incapacitated through grief to bargain effectively, and by devious methods keep hidden the costs of caskets, materials and the services they provide.

The following are the essential facts. Prices of funerals vary widely; among cultural groups, among families of different economic levels, among families within the same ethnic and economic groups, and among customers of one firm. The funeral director maintains that judgment should not be based in any one case on costs alone, and that other factors (to be recounted later) should be taken into account. Costs of funerals for categories of deceased individuals vary widely. Old age assistance burials are paid for by municipal governments in different states at differing prices; still born babies are buried with a minimum of service and materials at as low as nine dollars and prices up to several times that much; young chiidren at twenty-five dollars or much more; paupers on contract at practically no cost.

Prices offered by one firm, in general following the quality of the casket chosen, vary in specific instances from $100 to $6,000, from $250 to $25,000, from $100 to $650. The limits are determined in practice by the economic level of the clientele, the exigencies of bargaining, and in some measure by the locale. A study, reported by the managing director of the National Selected Morticians in 1954, involving 102,101 funerals in large cities and small towns throughout the United States, shows that 70 per cent cost less than $550, 23 per cent between $550 and $800, and seven per cent $800 or more. Slightly over seven per cent of funerals cost $200 or less. (5, pp. 34, 40, 41)

Studies made (1) in New York State by the International Business Machines Corporation for the New York State Funeral Directors Association, involving 14,513 cases, in 1946; (2) in Wisconsin by the Wisconsin Funeral Directors Association, involving the clients of 158 of its members, in 1952; and (3) in Massachusetts by the Massachusetts Funeral Directors Association, involving 6,292 cases in 1952, show that the price range in which the largest number of funerals fall was $401 to $500. In these studies the number of funerals costing less than $200 constituted 16 per cent in New York and 9 per cent in Wisconsin and Massachusetts. The study made in New York State shows that the price levels from $301 to $600 covered the cost of a smaller proportion of funerals in New York City than in the rest of the state. The reverse was true of funerals costing $601 to $1,000— i.e., a greater proportion of people paid the higher prices in the metropolis.

An oral statement in 1951 by the director of one of the national funeral directors associations gives the following minimum prices quoted for funerals in certain sections of the country:

Southern California	$ 70
The North	100
Chicago	135
New York	150
The South	110

These figures demonstrate clearly that costs of funerals vary greatly. The studies would be of more value if they indicated the family
incomes of the groups paying for funerals in the various price ranges.
Some slight approach to that problem can be made by considering
the expectations of families in the matter of costs of funerals.

According to the study made for the National Funeral Directors
Association in 1948, the average price considered reasonable by the
persons responding for the country was $527. (4, p. 29) We have
seen above that in at least three states the prices paid most frequently
in 1946 and 1952 fell within the range $401-$500, and in the study
of the National Selected Morticians seventy per cent of all funerals
cost less than $550. This comparison would indicate that the cus-
tomers pay much the same amounts as they consider reasonable, or
even less. If the figures fairly represent opinions of customers then
they believe they are faring very well indeed in the matter of costs
for funerals.

I do not find such gratification to be the case in many of the instances I have studied. I find very widespread feeling that costs are
much higher than they need to be; that undertakers do everything
in their power to raise them to the highest possible level; that dignified,
suitable funerals could be profitably provided at much less expense;
and that the choice by the consumer of the less costly funerals is made
difficult and disagreeable. Many who hold these sentiments also
realize that they will need to pay larger sums than they regard as
necessary or fair. In that sense only their expectations correspond
to the answers secured in the study for the National Funeral Directors
Association.

Much that has been written and spoken by unbiased critics about
funerals for decades past has indicated that funeral costs are unneces-
sarily high, and that they constitute a very great burden on all
families especially on those of the lower income groups. The classical
study on the subject was made in 1928, financed by an initial appro-
priation of $24,000, later supplemented, from the Metropolitan Life
Insurance Company. It was conducted under an Advisory Committee on Burial Survey composed of forty-one very distinguished social
workers, economists, clergymen of the three large religious groups,
educators, research workers, attorneys, psychiatrists, together with six
morticians from various parts of the country. (6) Statistical studies
were made of over 15,000 actual funeral bills, of which 2800 were
found in records of decedents' estates in New York, Brooklyn, Chicago

and Pittsburgh, 8800 in industrial policies throughout the United States, 3100 in claims for burial expenses filed with the United States Veterans Bureau, and 300 in widows' applications for pensions to the New York Board of Child Welfare.

The author of the study reported that, at that date (1928), excessive expenditures for funerals, particularly among low income groups, had been a matter of great concern to leaders in civic, religious and social work for over thirty years; that a two-year study under the Burial Reform Association had been made from 1894 to 1896, recommending simple funerals; and that a two-year study (1903 to 1905) was made by the New York Charity Organization Society, concluding with proposals for the correction of abuses.   That study listed as causes for excessive funeral expenditures among the poor: (1) mistaken pride, fear of what the neighbors might think, (2) desire "to do right by" the dead, (3) encouragement by unscrupulous undertakers, and (4) the fact that the family is in no condition to bargain.   Gebhart, the author, also reported a study undertaken in 1919 by the Chicago City Club, and later carried on by the Chicago Council of Social Agencies, showing burdensome costs of funerals.

The overwhelming evidence of the oppressive weight of funeral costs on families must be considered in relation to the selling methods of funeral directors, and the economic and social pressures which prompt these methods.   It must not be assumed that the undertaking industry could, under ordinary circumstances, maintain high prices so universally and over so great a stretch of time.   Neither must it be assumed that they gouge their clientele out of a simple desire to become wealthy quickly.   Later chapters will take up the subjects of economic and social pressures.   Selling methods and buyers' response need to be analyzed first.

Before the customer sits down with the undertaker to determine style of the funeral and to agree on costs, he has already given up the greatest bargaining asset that the buyer possesses in any transaction, namely, the privilege of declining all offers and seeking another seller. When he turned over the body to the funeral director he practically limited himself to that one practitioner.   Seldom, if ever, is a body taken by the family from one establishment to another because of dissatisfaction or disagreement over terms.   Moving the body to the funeral parlor in the first place is done by the undertaker as a matter of course.   The procedure is accepted by the family because of, first, its reliance on him for the proper steps to be taken and, second, because of the almost universal desire to have the body out of the living quarters.

By the time the representative of the family meets with the funeral director in the office of the latter, the preparation of the body has begun. The customer finds himself practically bound to find within the offerings made to him one that he will accept. This constitutes the major advantage secured by the funeral director: gaining possession of the body before coming to agreement on costs and style of funeral. There are other incidental advantages to him. He gets a look at the home when he comes to get the body and ask the preliminary questions. Thereby he gains an impression of the range of prices the customer is able to meet. He also makes sure that negotiations will take place in his office where he finds it easier to take command of the situation, sitting at his desk. The customer, meanwhile, adjusts his chair as required by the position of the undertaker. At the very outset of the actual negotiations, then, the funeral director has gained a very considerable strategic advantage.

The custom of charging for funerals according to the prices of the caskets involved is fairly general. The mark-up on the caskets runs from three to six times their cost to the funeral firm. Added to this price are such additional items as the customer may wish which have not entered into the base calculation. The method is an old one, going back to the days when the undertaker "undertook" the task which involved as chief cost that of the coffin. The method has been continued partly because of the difference between establishments of the relation of overhead to total costs, and also a reluctance to reveal to customers the exact number of items entering into total costs. For example, a director who takes care of an average of fifty funerals a year has something like one funeral a week as an average. His overhead, however, must be maintained at a level adequate for a volume of business much greater, and costs of funerals must be high enough to cover all expenses incurred. It avoids a great deal of "misunderstanding" on the part of the customer to make the casket cost the determinant of the total funeral price. The method has been attacked as a means of making allegedly high profits without giving the client the opportunity of making comparisons and calculations.

Actually the largest element in the retention of this method of pricing is the facility it affords the funeral director to set a total price for the funeral according to the standard of living of each family. There is strong conviction throughout the funeral directors' group that a family should arrange for a funeral on the level of its capacity to pay. This conviction is freely expressed by individual undertakers, by the booklets put out to attract patronage, by the funeral directors' associations in their publications, by the independent trade journals, by cemetery officials and by florists. This concept forms the basis of the sums to be allowed from estates for burial purposes by surrogate courts. Funeral directors defend the concept on the dual assumption that according to the accepted customs: (1) a family *should* spend a sum and present a display on a level appropriate to its status, and (2) the love and respect of the family for its dead is shown to the world by the quality of the funeral in terms of money spent. They express disbelief, disgust, or violent disapproval of standards contrary in effect to their assumptions. To ignore them is to go against "the American way of life," as they interpret it.

The persons who are quite unwilling to pay the prices for funerals ordinarily asked are to be found among all groups. The undertakers are fully aware that their contention that every family should provide display at a funeral commensurate with its income is not universally accepted. "Analysis" reports that almost a third of the respondents to a questionnaire think simple services are a good thing, 13 per cent because funerals are not an occasion for display, 9 per cent because they are easier on the family and relieve their feelings, 5 per cent because they save unnecessary expense, and 4 per cent because they avoid prolonged ceremony. (4, p. 15) A survey made at Texas Technological College in 1951 indicates that 67 per cent of all persons interviewed either were against elaborate funerals, or did not care one way or the other. Thirty-three per cent thought they deserved an expensive burial.

An important feature of the negotiations between customer and mortician is found in the display room in which caskets of various prices are exhibited. The funeral director may let the members of the family observe the caskets and their price labels without his presence, or may lead them from one article to another with constant explanations and selling arguments. It is not to be inferred, however, that the presence of the undertaker necessarily indicates that he is attempting to bring inordinate pressure on the customer to purchase in a higher price range than he intended or can afford. Instances can be cited in which the only effort made by the funeral director was to explain the difference in style and composition of caskets. It is not to be inferred either that all families desire to be left to their own devices in the crucial decision involved in the choice of casket. It is surely true that a very large number, and in my estimation a large majority, would much prefer to learn the costs of types of caskets, and to make their decision without persuasion by the seller.

The arrangement of caskets is almost invariably such that the higher priced caskets show up glamorously. In most display rooms the lowest priced casket is unfavorably shown, and is sometimes difficult to find without the help of the undertaker. To begin with the most expensive caskets are not always pointed out. The suggestion of high cost may discourage the customer. The cleverest device is outlined in a book intended for the member firms by the managing director of National Selected Morticians, Inc., Wilber M. Krieger. Krieger advises the funeral directors to divide the range of their selling price into quartiles and then to attempt to sell in the third quartile, or at prices above their median sales price. He had found that the "proper level" of the first group of caskets shown the customer is $125 to $150 above the median. The price does not scare the buyer, and from the reaction to the showing the funeral director may judge whether that level of prices is too high or too low. Then the customer should be shown a group of caskets providing great contrast in both price and quality, $5 to $25 below the median, if the buyer has given evidence he desires a lower priced article than those first shown. If the second group of caskets is unsatisfactory, the third (a "rebound unit") is shown at prices $5 to $25 above the median.

Krieger advises further that the buyer be led into a wide aisle prepared for the purpose, if on seeing the first group he has said nothing or asked for better caskets. In that aisle the top two quartiles are on exhibit, shown contrasting with each other. If the necessity arises of serving buyers who "must" purchase below the median price, they should be served "graciously and with just as much courtesy and attention" as one prepared to spend large sums. For the customer wanting a low priced casket, a narrow aisle leading to the left should have been arranged, not to "hide" these units, but merely because "less valuable space" has been used for them. This narrow aisle Krieger calls "Resistance Lane." (7, pp. 291-294)

The knowledge of the display room technique, so clearly revealed by Krieger, arouses a feeling of rebellion among many of the critics of the undertaker. It is, however, not a hidden device. By some individual buyers it has been welcomed as a way in which they could most clearly discriminate between the attractions of the various caskets and relate them to the sum of money they had to spend. In addition, it is obviously a technique that in general is often utilized in some form by commercial enterprises wherever displays are shown. The clients who have responded to inquiries in the course of this study have, for the most part, accepted the idea that there is manipulation by the seller involved in any appeal to the prospective buyer. The bargaining funeral situation is, however, different from the ordinary transaction. The funeral situation is one which coerces the family into action without the usual safeguards for the customer. The purchase of a casket is in no way comparable to the purchase of groceries, a new dress, golf sticks, or a coffee table for the living room.

It is the extraordinary features of bargaining for the funeral goods and services that form the loop hole in which the customer loses his usual protections and the undertaker finds special negotiating advantages. In general the undertaker attempts to utilize his advantage by telling his client what he should do and how much he should pay. Usually he holds that in doing so he is rendering a service and conferring a favor. The assumption that it is his function to determine the total price does not stop at the point at which he persuades the customer what items to choose, but goes further to justify determining one price for an article or service for one person and a higher price for a different person, especially one of greater financial means. The undertaker assumes that an obligation rests on the responsible person to pay a total cost commensurate with the financial status of the deceased. A device clearly illustrating the assumption, as well as the clever implementation of it, is to be seen in the procedure that is followed by some "progressive" firms. They itemize costs rather than charge according to price of the casket.

Here is an illustration of such an operation. The undertaker sits down with the customer and shows him a printed list of items and services involved in the conduct of the funeral. There appears first the newspaper obituary item on which the funeral director makes no profit. He tells the client what the rates are for all the papers in which the item might appear, letting the client decide the number of insertions to appear and the papers in which they are to appear. The total sum for all insertions provides an index to the funeral director of the client's ability and willingness to pay for other items. If the total sum for newspaper items amounts to a relatively high figure as compared with the sums determined upon by previous customers, then the undertaker gets his first clue that the client can pay the highest rates for items on a sliding scale.

Second, the undertaker gains further insight into the customer's capacity to pay by taking up certain other items that involve no return to him. Third, the undertaker turns to the items on which his firm gets a small commission, say ten per cent on floral pieces. Fourth, he turns to items of his services and on these he sets prices that accord with his judgment of the customer's ability to pay. Last, he takes the family representatives into the display room refraining from urging of any kind, and allows them to choose from all the caskets, with prices clearly marked. He first shows them caskets of the price range he thinks they should pay. The caskets prices are marked up 100%, not three to six times the cost to him. He regards the method as fair and honest, more ethical than the "unit price" plan, i.e., that of setting the total cost of the funeral according to the price of the casket.

The concept of providing funerals at low cost and attracting volume of patronage by so doing, is rarely found except among the establishments of "the advertising" funeral directors. While the non-advertising funeral directors comprise many who deride advertising as unethical in their business, none of them sees anything unethical in the manipulation of customers as described above.

Whether by conscious design or not, funeral directors take great pains to keep the customer within narrow confines of choice during the bargaining period. Advertising not only presents a choice to the client in his selection of undertaker, but it also gives him something of an idea of cost. It provides the concept of a basic price for the article he is to buy, since the advertising funeral directors frequently name the minimum cost of a funeral in their advertisements. The whole idea of setting a uniform price for specific goods and services is in direct opposition to the policy of determining prices for each particular customer according to what he can afford to pay.

The practice of advertising funeral bargains as bait to lure customers into buying high priced caskets (the so-called "bait advertising") has been condemned by the funeral directors' associations and by practically all the individual firms. It does exist, but not to any great extent. It is not followed by all the advertising funeral directors as has sometimes been charged. It is a device of the fringe of flagrantly unethical practitioners that admittedly exists in the funeral business.

One circumstance that makes the undertaker rigid in his attitude

toward remuneration for materials and services is his inability to reclaim the casket or plot after burial. There is no question but that
he would be faced with many an unpaid bill of large dimensions if
he did not protect himself. The testimony of those who knew the
business methods and hazards of the old fashioned undertaker amply
proves that without rigid caution on this score many funeral directors
would be ruined. The argument that every one is entitled to a decent
funeral does not logically lead to the conclusion that the funeral
director should take risks in the matter of payment.

Popular magazine writers and others have said rightly that the
funeral director tries to find out all the assets of the customer and
then charges him accordingly. Serious evils of overcharging do exist
in the funeral industry. Nevertheless the desire of the undertaker to
know where his money is coming from when he accepts a funeral, is
not always an indication that he is attempting to appropriate all the
property of the family. The remedy for "the sucker funeral" in which
a family is charged several times the worth of the goods furnished
and the services rendered, and for the exploitation that occurs when
the purchaser is induced by one or another form of pressure to agree
to a price equal to his total belongings, does not lie in hiding assets
from the undertaker. Many years ago the Metropolitan Life Insurance Company discovered that fact when it ordered its agents
never to reveal to funeral directors the amount of insurance held by
the bereaved family, and later realized the futility of the measure.

Because he must make sure at the beginning that he will be paid,
the undertaker insists on a definite understanding of the methods of
payment, whether by cash, life insurance, funeral insurance, government payments, mortuary credit plan, bank loan, or payments from
an estate.

One idiosyncracy of a few morticians in their relations with families of the dead is puzzling. It is the habit of making charges on the
bill as finally submitted at rates far higher than current prices. A related practice is also to be found, of charging for items that were not
furnished, such as items necessary only in a burial, when actually the
body has been cremated. An illustration of listing items at uncom-
monly high prices is to be seen in the bill of a funeral director who,
when arranging for the preparation of the body, had refused to use
one of the many shirts possessed by the deceased. He purchased a
shirt of the same make and size, used it, and charged precisely five
times the standard price.

The funeral director, faced with such a complaint, or talked to later about that sort of occurrence, seldom advances the defense of clerical error, nor admits any lack of business acumen. He often says there is no relation between the price of shirts on the store counter, and shirts provided in his preparation room. In fairness it must be said that he pays unusual prices for materials he secures from firms providing mortuary supplies. He believes, too, that for customers the cost of the shirt is a minor matter in view of the importance of the occasion on which it is to be worn. The thing that counts, in his estimation, is the judgment exercised in dressing the body artistically for the last look of relatives and friends. Under the explanations given for any extraordinary pricing practice there always seems to lie a curious but apparently honest assumption, that undertakers follow rules of their own making, chief of which is that it is their prerogative to decide what the buyer should pay.

In the negotiations between buyer and undertaker, the latter stresses the lasting comfort that comes from the last look at the face of the deceased. His argument is aided by the force of the traditional practice of viewing the remains. As has been stated in Chapter II the weight of authoritative evidence is heavily against the probability that the last glimpse of the dead and "restored" face will provide any basis for a "memory image." Even if it did, it would be unfortunate if what is seen in the casket should blot out the more pleasant images of previous associations. Nevertheless, the alleged solace for the bereaved to come from this incident strengthens materially the funeral director's urging that the body be retained above ground for three or more days. There then ensues the need for embalming, restoring and adorning the body with expensive casket and accoutrements, as well as for all the succeeding stages of a "fine funeral."

The majority of families accept the custom because they are led to believe it is the only proper procedure, and because in their grief and guilt they are anxious to insure a sense of satisfaction within themselves that they have given all that could be asked. It is questionable whether, at the time of bargaining, a large number of them might not decide differently if they were more adequately advised. The great number who now comply under the pressure of the circumstances and the advice they get, but who later complain about the gruesome practice and the painful dragging out of the final leave taking, certainly would not agree to the elaborate process.

There are two reasons for disagreement with it. The first is that there is no necessity for the extensive preparation and proceedings. If the body is disposed of promptly, embalming and all the rest of the preparation is not required. Any necessary religious rites connected with burial can be performed then as well as later. The second involves the whole question of the method of adjustment to the reality of bereavement. The separation has come; the loved one is dead; the problem is then that of facing the future.

It is clear to the minds of many who have thought the question through that facing the future is not aided by hanging on to the dead, physical remains and decking them out in ephemeral glory. Rather, this emphasis on the body hinders the acquisition of the deeper acceptance of the present fact and determination to make the most of the future. The more there is of emphasis on rational procedures to insure emotional adjustment, the better; the more emphasis on reassessment of the values in life and the spiritual aspects involved in it the better.

The funeral directors have much to say about one other item in the negotiations with bereaved families. It is the advice they give not only on the funeral, the burial plot to select, and other relevant matters, but also on a long list of questions, concerns, or anxieties quite outside the business in hand. First among them is the whole category of money matters: insurance, government benefits, making a will, even the selection of investment opportunities. Second is the large group of personal problems, for which the competence of undertakers to advise will be treated in a later chapter. They include especially the selection of a clergyman to officiate at the funeral. Advice, when volunteered by the undertaker may irritate or anger, as in cases in which solace is persistently expressed and not appreciated.

Summary. A few basic features of the bargaining process between the bereaved family and the funeral director stand out among the complex factors that have been described. First, the situation is not comparable to the usual buyer-seller relationship, despite one of the defenses of the undertaker that he is following customary business practices. On both sides many strong irrational factors enter, and the result cannot be characterized as a reasoned weighing of costs against rationally conceived benefits. Dominating the thoughts of many clients, guilt and grief seek for display of a costly nature to lend prestige to the dead one and to the family at a time of critical public attention. The extraordinary need of the undertaker for more "cases" induces him to magnify the family's desire for show of status and consequent increased revenue for him. The stage is then set for expenditures up to and beyond the capacity of the family to meet them.

The undertaker replies to critics that there is no compulsion on the buyer. Nevertheless the pressures on him are great. The need to act quickly is one of them. He finds himself facing unusual responsibilities in a situation that isolates him while he is subject to pressure from within himself and from the undertaker. His lack of knowledge of what to do in the rare event that has occurred puts him at a serious disadvantage. The technical abilities of the undertaker are not great, and yet there is no criteria known to the client by which he can judge the money value of materials and services he buys. The total expenditures are determined largely by the other party to the bargain, and even comparison of charges by different firms is not open to him. The undertaker persists in his self-assumed right to use all possible, lawful means to induce expenditures up to the level that he assumes proper according to the client's station in life and ultimate capacity to pay.

The fact that the costs of funerals are tragically burdensome in many instances is minimized by the funeral director. He maintains that the satisfaction of "a fine funeral," compensates the bereaved family for its cost. He maintains further that all expenses bear heavily on the poor; funerals do not differ from any other necessary large expenditure in this respect. The sum seems great, he says, because it comes from a sudden need; any necessary cost realized suddenly is painful to meet. He claims credit for charitable works, since he says he furnishes funerals at no cost at all when, occasionally, a family cannot pay. The costs of labor and materials for charity cases must be added to the average prices paid for other funerals. He admits freely that there are "chiseling" practitioners who exploit, and maintains that complaints against him are due to their activities.

Relief from the trying experience of the negotiations on funeral costs lies open to the client in two directions. One is in making arrangements for the funeral long before the need for it arises. Pre-arrangements can be effected for one's own funeral, and by so doing the influence of grief and guilt can be avoided and time can be gained for comparison of prices of different establishments. The other avenue of relief is that of simple and immediate disposal of the body, and a deliberate turning to the deeper and more lasting adjustment to the loss through emphasis on the spiritual aspects of the crisis.

CHAPTER VI

INSTITUTIONAL RELATIONSHIPS

All we ask is to be let alone.
JEFFERSON DAVIS

The funeral director's responsibilities bring him into contact with several community agencies. Among them are, the medical profession, nursing, local government, the church, and, occasionally, private welfare agencies. It is important for the present study to determine the degree to which his duties involve him in the processes of these agencies.

Respect For the Physician. The funeral director gets some of his cases by referral from physicians and nurses. Many of the attacks on him include the charge that he recompenses them with money for such favors. Reasons other than monetary compensation are advanced when a doctor or nurse is questioned about referring cases to only one or a few undertakers. Each one may say that he has referred cases only to the firms he did because of: his knowledge of a limited number of firms; confidence in the integrity of one or few and ignorance of others; desire to send cases of minority group members to undertakers of the same groups; assurance of the suitability of the price range of the funeral directors referred to; mutual friendship; blood relationship; or common bond of religion with the undertaker. Pure habit may be the basis of selection by a nurse or physician. Funeral directors, when questioned, will not admit that they have ever given financial remuneration, although they sometimes raise the question whether or not harm would result to any one if they were to do so.

Favors of other than monetary nature are admittedly given by some practitioners to key persons, including clergymen who might direct cases to them. An article in a trade journal brings out the controversial nature of the practices: "It has always been our opinion that giving gifts at Christmas time or at any other time, by morticians to doctors, nurses, ministers or any other groups of individuals is wrong. . . . Now that industrial firms are beginning to question the wisdom of such a policy, many of our profession should seriously review their reasons for so doing." (1, p. 28)

Strong disapproval of fee splitting between funeral director and physician is expressed in the codes of ethics of the funeral directors' associations. The practice is forbidden in the licensing provisions of most of the states. The prominence of the prohibition, however, justifies a presumption that the practice exists in some quarters.

The relation of the undertaker to the professional persons in the matter of referrals of cases is superficial at best. Little or no information about the deceased and his family is given to the mortician and no standard practices are followed as in social work referrals. Often, however, clergymen of all faiths ask for special consideration for families whom they have known when referring them to funeral directors. The relation of the clergyman to the undertaker is a closer one than that of the nurse or physician, as will be shown in later pages.

The undertaker's role relates him to the physician in slight measure, inasmuch as it is his duty to get the certificate of death signed by the latter and to file it with the proper health authority. Legally, it is the responsibility of the physician to file the certificate, but the duty is universally regarded as part of the routine of the funeral director. The accuracy of official records is the focal point of concern in the matter of filing the death certificate and securing the burial permit. The burden of the law is to assure certainty before burial that death has occurred and that it has occurred from natural causes. Since the official record may become a vital factor in a possible legal contest, its accuracy is regarded as a serious matter. An error, such as mistakenly filing in a district other than that in which the death has occurred, may cause considerable difficulty for the undertaker, including threat of or actual loss of license.

Respect and good will characterize the attitude of funeral directors toward physicians. Indeed, more of them would aspire to the practice of medicine than to any other single occupation. This is probably because they have had a taste of the kind of preparation and training the physician goes through, and also because, in a minor way, embalming involves medical knowledge. Occasionally an undertaker criticizes doctors for issuing death certificates that he regards as erroneous. However, serious charge is seldom made. On the whole, relations between funeral directors and physicians are casually cooperative.

Use of Government Agencies. There are three chief respects in which funeral directors are related to government officials. The first has to do with the advice given to clients in the matter of benefits and proceedings of which they may not have been aware. These include old age insurance for surviving spouses and children under eighteen years of age, old age assistance, veterans rights, and local welfare benefits. Advice is given also on matters in which government agencies may be involved, such as procedures in respect to wills, laws of inheritance, and settling estates. The advice that is given involves only a limited knowledge of social security, welfare, and law; but, coming at the time it does, it is important. Undertakers vary widely in their acquaintance with the governmental and legal matters involved and in their skill in interpreting them.

The second manner in which the funeral director is related to government officials is in the same area as the first, namely, the follow up to see that benefits are secured by the family. Often he seeks out assistance benefits in order to insure payment for the funeral, or to obtain a larger sum for a funeral than he could otherwise secure. The undertaker is entitled to a sum from social security or welfare funds that will bring his total renumeration up to the minimal cost for a funeral. However, three questions present themselves in practice: What is a fair minimal price for a funeral? Has the funeral director secured more for himself than the maximum amount allows? Has he secured funds for a family not legally entitled to them?

The type of charges heard against the undertaker in this area is illustrated by the report of the Attorney General of New York State to the State Commissioner of Health and Social Welfare on December 28, 1954. In it he relates the procedures and findings of a year long study, "resulting from numerous complaints both from official sources and the general public charging unscrupulous behavior" on the part of the funeral service industry. Records covering 602 funerals were scrutinized during the study and more than fifty funeral directors were examined under oath. The following statements are taken from the report:

"Welfare recipients will often assign assets, such as insurance policies, to their Welfare Districts. . . . In New York City, if the cost of the funeral is not more than $500, the City will contribute up to $250 out of the assigned assets toward the bill if there are no other funds available. . . . If the assigned assets exceed the total welfare payments made to the deceased, the $250 is being paid out of funds which would otherwise be restored to the deceased's estate. On the other hand if the assets are less than the payments made to the deceased, the $250 is being paid out of funds which belong to the city and state, the latter by virtue of its sharing in the relief costs. . . . In Districts outside the City of New York the policy is generally the same, except that the $250 figure varies between $175 and $315 and, in many cases there is no provision for limitation on the total cost of the funeral.

"An unscrupulous segment of the undertaking industry has found a fertile field for fraud in these procedures.

"Disciplinary action against seven undertakers has already been recommended to the State Department of Health. Numerous others are now being processed for similar disciplinary action and possible criminal prosecution." (2)

Among the several accounts of actions of funeral directors, which either sought duplicate payment from different sources for the same, or part of the same bill, or which resulted in depriving the city and state of sums due it, is the following:

"In another case the same undertaker issued three bills for a single funeral. One, to the family of the deceased for $362.02. Second to the Department of Welfare for $202. Third, to the Social Security Agency for $363.06. He also submitted two affidavits to the Department of Welfare indicating that the agreed price of the funeral was $202 and that he was unpaid. Actually, evidence showed he received duplicate payment for identical charges from the family and the Department of Welfare. In addition, he again helped to defraud both city and state of the lump sum death benefit due them from the Social Security Agency.

" . . . The hard and cold fact is that many (such) persons of limited economic means obtain funerals which cost even less than $175. . . . I find it difficult to justify the higher sum ($250) paid for the funeral of a recipient of public assistance." (*Idem*)

The Attorney General recommended that studies be made with the aim of: (1) reviewing the figure at which reimbursement is made by welfare districts, putting a limitation on supplementation by the family, (2) codifying rules of departments of social welfare to close all loopholes for the unscrupulous operators and to make it clear that any violation of the Public Health Law has been made with intent to defraud, (3) providing an administrative checking system to make it possible to supervise efficiently the payment of welfare funds, (4) considering the advisability of designating a Deputy Commissioner of Health to supervise the pertinent sections of the Public Health Law.

A typical reply immediately came from the funeral service industry, in large part maintaining that no sweeping conclusions as to the entire industry could logically be drawn from as few as 602 cases; that prices of everything are so high that the costs of entire funerals quoted by the Attorney General were not excessive; and that the "whole situation has been handled in an entirely unfair manner." (3, p. 15)

It seems safe to conclude that, while it is fair for funeral directors to use all legitimate means to secure for the bereaved families and for themselves the sums intended for minimal funerals from public funds established for the purpose, still the number of cases involving improper manipulation of public funds is large enough to warrant further protective measures against the guilty minority of undertakers.

The third respect in which undertaking relates itself to government is found in the many instances in which funeral directors become the public officials controlling the governmental supervision over themselves and their colleagues. State boards setting the standards for the examining and licensing of funeral directors are usually made up largely of funeral directors, since presumably they are the individuals who have knowledge of the good and bad practices. In such circumstances the possibility exists of using the authority possessed by the members of such boards of licensing examiners to favor one individual or group over another. In more than one state the charge has been made by responsible persons representing religious and cooperative groups, that organization to foster funeral provision by groups organized on a mutual basis have been frustrated by funeral directors acting in official capacities.

The point that undertaking is prone to become a law unto itself is given emphasis by the extent to which funeral directors and embalmers constitute the membership of state boards which direct the administration of the laws concerning themselves. In the majority of states more than half or all of the members must be experienced and licensed operators, and in some an official of the state department of health is the only other member. (In at least three states, however, the state board of health is the agency administering legislative provisions for the control of undertaking.) In four states the influence

of the organized undertakers reaches furthest in the provision of the
law that only members of the private state funeral directors' association are to be appointed to the official state board of embalmers
and funeral directors.

Disregard of Social Work. In the preceding section it was seen
that undertakers have dealings with public welfare agencies when the
family of the deceased has been on relief. There is another way in
which the fields of welfare and undertaking relate to each other, as
when the customer of the funeral director is a client of a social agency.
Potentially the two fields are also related when the customer of the
undertaker is in need of aid or counseling by a trained social worker.

Funeral directors, as a rule, give advice on a "common sense" basis,
to the families with which they deal. When the funeral director advises families that are clients of social agencies he may be following
a line opposed to the advice of the social workers involved, or he may
be dealing in an unprofessional way with families who need professional advice. The funeral director's counseling is given in the context of an emergency. That emergency would be only one of many
factors that any social worker would have in mind in helping a family
to self-disciplined adjustment of a more permanent nature.

From the standpoint of professional social work, the agency dealing
with the family in question should be consulted about the arrangements for the funeral. There is very little referral of families to appropriate agencies by funeral directors, and small understanding on
the part of the undertakers of the kinds of service given, or methods
used by the agencies.

In the smaller communities, or in cases in which the undertaker
knows the family personally, he may be aware of its long-term needs.
Under such circumstances he may take its need into account in the
advice he gives, even in few instances recommending less expensive
funerals than those desired. In the case of more impersonal connections with clients, however, the undertaker does not normally take
account of the total family situation or its prospects for the future.
Very often he is ignorant of the sort of help that is available through
professional social work channels. When challenged with the statement that his usefulness would be extended by acquaintance with
social work activities and methods sufficient to justify referral, his
most frequent reaction is an affirmation of his faith in "the training
school of hard knocks," and his distrust of the professional social
worker.

His attitude can be understood, not only because of the limitations of his training along social and psychological lines, but more particularly because of the isolation from community affairs that characterizes the funeral industry in all its phases. This latter factor has led to a further reason for the mortician's usual dislike of professionals and professionalism in social work, namely, the criticism of him sometimes offered by social workers, especially those assigned to neighborhoods of the lower economic levels. Some of the social workers, he complains, are arbitrary and, wherever possible, refuse to have anything to do with him.

Social workers, in turn, express great concern over the effect on poorer families of the high costs of funerals. They complain of three results brought about, in part at least, by lack of competent counseling in the planning of funerals. They are disruption of continuing self support, unsuccessful readjustment between members of the family, and failure to maintain a sense of long range values.

Occasionally, an exception to the customary lack of good relations is to be found. Funeral directors who are closely identified with a religious or ethnic group which sustains family service maintain better, and often very cooperative, relations. Inclusion of representation by a funeral director in a council of social agencies, though rare, serves to develop understanding through him between the funeral industry and welfare institutions.

In summary, it is clear that undertaking, although frequently in need of cooperation with the system of welfare agencies in the community, usually operates without regard to them.

Coexistence With the Clergy. The relation of undertaking to the church is of a different kind and on a different level from its relations to other community institutions. The funeral director relates himself, in a more or less perfunctory way to physician and to certain public officials. His relation to social workers is largely negative, due to a conflict of vocational spheres of influence with mutual clients and a conflict of techniques of counseling. With the clergy the relationship is one historically of longer duration, and is personally closer. The conflict that exists is a very fundamental one, lying on the level of the deepest values, and reflecting the opposition of secular and religious ideals. Although the roles of the funeral director and the clergyman are complementary in the conduct of the funeral, and despite the usual surface good relations between individuals, there is a fundamental conflict that lies deep and is widespread.

The opposing points of view become apparent to the observer in the jealousy felt on both sides in the matter of the one to whom the family turns first in time of death. The initial counseling of the bereaved person or family throws great weight not only to the decision of the other party selected and the procedures to be followed, but also to the depth of meaning of the ritual itself. The funeral directors offer to assist in the selection of the minister, priest or rabbi to officiate. Most of them make it known that they have on file the names of the clergymen of the various faiths and denominations in the town or city. The factors which motivate them to suggest specific names will appear later.

Not all clergymen will recommend specific undertakers to be engaged; some adhere rigidly to a hands off policy in order to avoid any appearance of partiality, and to keep themselves and their churches clear of involvement in the accusations made against undertakers. Among those who disapprove most heartily of the aims and methods of funeral directors are a number who keep themselves out of the struggle, and also a number who advise clients strongly whom to choose for burial service and whom to avoid.

All manner of relations exist between representatives of each group. The greatest mutual respect and friendship is often found, especially when the funeral director is a member of the church or synagogue in question. Complete indifference on a personal level and casual or automatic cooperation during the funeral is found as frequently. There are also cases of dislike and prolonged warfare in which the undertaker advises his customers to avoid the help of the clergyman in the funeral, and the same sort of treatment is accorded him in turn by the clergymen.

An understanding of the causes underlying the conflict will best be secured by a brief analysis of the point of view of each party in turn. The clergy regard the funeral as an integral and essential part of their function. They vary in the degree to which it is regarded by them as a duty for them to perform without consideration of a monetary kind from the family served. Many ministers are willing to officiate without pay; some say so in printed statements to parishioners. The remuneration they receive is usually intended for them and not as a contribution to the church. The same is true of Jewish synagogues. A Catholic church, on the other hand, may require that fees paid the priest be put into a fund, only a portion of which goes to him. Frequently a scale of prices is announced and the parishioner chooses at a fixed sum the type of services he wishes.

There is a fairly common recognition, however, of the parishioner's privilege to select the clergyman to officiate, despite the fact that church members in good standing seldom go outside their own institutions. Selection of the clergyman becomes an important item in the relationship of undertaker and minister or rabbi when the family has not remained constant in church attendance. It is in these families which do not claim any specific church affiliation that difficulties arise in largest measure. Clergymen are called upon frequently to serve families in these categories. Each service rendered requires a very considerable amount of time taken out of a crowded schedule.

In areas of new population, in which families have not made new church connections, the problem becomes acute. Clergymen are considered essential for the funeral service when all other church facilities can be ignored or postponed by families who have moved. For the clergy the request to serve non-members is often welcomed as a possible beginning of church connection, but it is also a vivid reminder that the modern mobility of families and the trend to secularization in urban society are lessening the hold of the church. The percentage of calls from non-members may run as high as eighty out of the total calls for funeral service. In communities which have experienced recent population growth the percentage of requests to the funeral director that he secure the clergyman's services has, in several instances, grown from fifteen or twenty to more than fifty in fifteen years or less.

The continuous repetition of these requests becomes a drain on the leader of a house of worship. The almost inevitable consequence is resentment for the whole undertaking business. Irritation, whenever it is felt, is aggravated further by the size of the payment that is customarily given for funeral services by non-members of churches. Five dollars is received more often than any other amount, ten dollars is the next most frequent sum. Remuneration in three figures occurs in well-to-do communities.

The managing director of the National Selected Morticians, Inc. has suggested twenty-five dollars as an average honorarium. He and others have noted that the officiating clergyman has to prepare a talk, and has to spend a great deal of time at the service and on the trip to the cemetery. The clergyman, when he compares the fee he has received with the total cost of the funeral, finds little reason for egotistical satisfaction. Few clergymen waste much time in remorse on that score, but some do find cause for sorrow in the realization that the church and the values for which it stands have been regarded as of very minor significance.

The last straw is piled on the clergyman's burden of chagrin in the knowledge that the undertaker may have named the sum to be paid to him. Often it is charged to the family as an item on the funeral bill and paid to the minister, priest, or rabbi by the funeral director. The clergyman invariably regards the funeral as a religious rite. He feels that the undertaker should take the part his function calls for and no more. In Catholic church services and those of Orthodox Jewish synagogues (usually those of the Conservative group also) there is little question as to the dominant influence at a funeral; it is the priest or rabbi. However, among the Protestants and in other groups, when the funeral services are held in the undertaking parlor, the control is largely in the hands of the funeral director. Even from Orthodox rabbis complaint is occasionally heard that the funeral director does not follow the prescribed conventions.

Clergymen of all faiths are often alarmed when they witness the exaggeration of the importance of the physical remains in comparison with the spiritual aspects of the funeral. They deplore the assumption by undertakers of sanctity for certain physical processes and materialistic phases of the ritual. Many also disapprove of the elaborate show at funerals encouraged by undertakers.

One example is to be found in the *Southern Funeral Director* for November, 1951. In an advertisement the smoke from an incense jar forms the heading "Reverence" against a line drawing of the Taj Mahal. Underneath are these words: "More and more are people coming everywhere to understand the ancient truth that Funeral Service—in its very essence—is a Service of *Reverent Refinement. . . .* And so it is that the Embalming of a family's Loved One is something vastly more than a 'mere technical operation.' In a very real sense, Embalming is a service of true reverence . . . the very essence of refined Funeral Practice." (4, p. 7)

An occasional occurrence that also aggravates the irritation of a minister is the holding of a funeral during church hours on Sunday. This seems to indicate a lack of consideration of the predominant interest of the church in the ritual, as well as a lack of regard for the claim of the church on those hours of its parishioners.

Turning to the attitude of the undertaker toward the clergyman, one usually finds an assumption that the funeral is the business of the former, particularly when the family has come to the undertaker first. The undertaker's strong tendency is to take over all details and to assume complete control. When the clergyman has been consulted by the family prior to the request that he officiate, the undertaker's attitude reveals more gratitude for the case, and more consideration for the clergyman's wishes.

Funeral directors respect church membership when the client asks that a clergyman be approached for him. Several funeral directors say they select clergymen whom they know, including in many instances ministers in their own churches. Several answer that they choose clergymen whose habit it is to keep their remarks very brief. In a few instances comes the answer: "I select a minister who needs the money." When stipulation of the amounts to be paid for the various types of masses has been made by a Catholic church, the priests express no dissatisfaction when the funeral director collects the money and sees that it reaches them.

Leaders in the industry urge fair play on the part of individual morticians in their dealings with clergymen. Occasionally a distinct note of condescension is heard from the undertakers in their defensive moments.

In the foreword to a publication of the National Funeral Directors Association these words appear: "It has, therefore, come as a shock and disappointment to many that . . . public attacks against the activities of the funeral directing profession have been given such great prominence in so many publications and have been, in a number of instances, spearheaded by members of the clergy, a group who more than any other has been the recipient of much of the promotional and charitable work of the funeral directing profession." (5, p. 2) In all probability this writer had in mind the occasions on which undertakers have made provision from funeral expenses for payments to needy clergymen, or have made contributions to church bazaars, or, more likely still, to cases of charity referred to them by clergymen. However, the words are obviously a leak in the reservoir of their resentment and are of the kind to arouse hostility among clergymen.

It is clear that the funeral director looks on the funeral as his domain. To understand the element of arbitrary possessiveness that so often characterizes his attitude, it is helpful to look at two examples of funerals that are typical. In the first case a family came to a funeral home in an underprivileged area, made arrangements for a funeral costing approximately three hundred fifty dollars. It was the father who had died in his late fifties. Neither he nor any member had belonged to a church. They stated that his mother had been a Methodist, and they asked that the funeral director secure the services of a minister of any denomination. They agreed to pay the minister's fee in addition to the three hundred and fifty dollars. The funeral director attempted to induce a Methodist minister to come, but failed. He found a Baptist minister who agreed to come for five dollars.

Ten minutes before the hour for the funeral service the minister came. He listened to a brief description from the funeral director, of the life and family of the deceased, met the members of the family, and immediately began the service. It consisted of a prayer, a Scripture reading and a ten-minute sermon in which he admonished them to be thankful for the modest but good life of the father and for their long association with him. He urged them to realize that death comes to all men and advised them to adjust to a family life without the father. Since he was not to go on the long ride to a cemetery outside the city, he stood before the casket and recited the committal of the body to the ground, "dust to dust" and all, and left.

In this instance the family was fully satisfied. They were not religious, they said, but they believed it was proper to have a prayer and a sermon at a funeral. They accepted the cost of the funeral as inevitable, and they wanted a minister at as little cost to them as possible. There was no complaint or dissatisfaction from the family or from the minister. The critical observer may deplore the family's lack of church loyalty, the high cost of the funeral, or the disparity in the amounts of payment of undertaker and minister. Nevertheless there are many who, like this family, are not close to a church and who do not desire to be, but who because of tradition, present custom, or memory of family habits in the past, still want a minister to be brought in. In these cases the undertaker has not preempted the prerogatives of the minister; he has merely stepped into a gap the clergy are not filling, and is maintaining connection between the bereaved families and the church.

Another factor affecting the relations of the clergy and undertakers consists of the growth of contemporary reliance on experts. When death comes these families turn to one whom they regard as an expert for the occasion—an undertaker. Having found an expert, they are inclined to follow passively the advice offered them and to make little or no active effort to look further.

The clergyman's importance at the funeral is lessened by the family's lack of strong conviction of any kind in the face of death, or the conflict of basic religious attitudes among the acquaintances of the famly who are in attendance. Consider a second example of a funeral in which the undertaker secured, at the request of the family, a clergyman to "officiate." It took place in an elegantly furnished funeral home of an upper class community. The mother in a family of four had died and the father had arranged for a funeral up to, if not beyond, the amount the family could afford. Relatives and friends numbering approximately thirty met, and then sat quietly in something of a circle around the casket. They varied widely in religious commitments, in political and economic views, and in matters of family living. The family members had attended no church but had asked the funeral director to engage a clergyman. When the clergyman arrived he was ushered to the rostrum by the funeral director and introduced. He immediately proceeded to read a large number of scattered Biblical passages without explanation or interpretation. The passages covered a large range of subjects and were excerpts from diverse social and historical contexts. After the reading and a prayer he departed, and the service was ended. There was practically no significance for any one present except by possible incidental past connection with one or another passage that was read.

The net result was a large expenditure by the family for the funeral, a brief gesture toward tradition in the form of Scripture readings and a prayer, and a brief gathering involving little intercommunication between persons with no common interest. It was in no sense a ritual. A stilted and slightly boring experience had been had by all. It is difficult to devise a meaningful funeral service under such circumstances. Perhaps the friendly manner of the funeral director and the slightly elegant appointments of the room were all that could logically be provided. It had been a "nice" service, in the shallowest sense of that term. The question remaining uppermost in the mind of the observer after such an experience is, not what has the undertaker done to the funeral to rob it of meaning, nor what could any clergyman do to put deep meaning into it, but rather why hold such a service at all.

The relation between undertaking and the church is revealed in a more intense light in the public struggles that have occurred. Three will be cited. In 1937 the Ministers' Association in Middletown, New York, agreed upon a set of principles and procedures to be followed at funerals, most of which were at odds with the usual practices of funeral directors. The type of reaction and the alignment of forces in the subsequent struggle is described in the *Christian Century* by the Reverend Hugh Stevenson Tigner:

"When our ideas were published . . . two months later . . . the reaction was immediate, spontaneous and wholly unexpected. . . . Our act was reported in newspapers throughout the eastern part of the United States. The town buzzed as I never knew a town to buzz. . . .

"The nature of the response was bitterly hostile. . . . Many agreed but had no reason for making any noise. . . . I know of no criticism or objection by anyone who attended our churches on the day we started our case. . . . Officially nothing happened . . . the undertakers decided to turn the matter over to the regional association. . . . Out-of-town clergymen were called in for funerals whenever the family would allow it.

"Least of all did we foresee that the general business community would regard our action as bordering upon subversion. . . . The reasoning is thus: **Any existing and** clearly unforbidden business is sacred. A thing may be **morally** reprehensible, but that is merely an unpractical argument against it. If it is a legitimate business, that gives it absolute authority . . . churches are expected to function in whatever system secular interests provide." (6, p. 1262)

About ten years later, the minister in the Congregational Church in Elgin, Illinois, took the lead in a pronouncement by the Ministerial Association of the practices ideally to be followed at funerals from a Christian point of view. It, too, was at variance with the habits and the convictions of the undertakers. Intense feeling was aroused and some effort made to bring about an understanding between the two groups. There was no open fight, and the issue was resolved in small part. Essentially it has remained as a distinct difference in attitudes and values. (7, pp. 1-4)

In 1953 the parish social relations committee of the Holy Trinity Episcopal Church in Oxford, Ohio, made a study "of the increasing secular encroachment on the marriage and burial practices in the United States" which attracted wide notice. Well over eighty-five per cent of the members of the church approved the recommendations of the study. Hundreds of letters were received as a result of the published account in *Time* magazine and the Associated Press coverage;

these letters expressed "a great many related personal distressing experiences that the writers had endured during the crisis of a death in
the family . . . some vigorous . . . protests from funeral homes and
national agencies (including some virtually irrational statements) . . .
distressing accounts of commercial pressure (concern for fees) on the
part of clergymen . . . (word from) five or six funeral directors of
their agreement that steps toward reform were being made." (8, p. 2)

The statements made by the churches in these three towns represent
the point of view of the most aggressive element among the clergy.
The majority of ministers would subscribe, in part at least, to the
main emphases embodied in the three statements. Items included in
each one of the statements relate (1) to planning by the minister and
family together as an initial step, (2) to closing the casket before the
service begins. Items mentioned in two of the statements include:
(1) no charge for church or minister's services; (2) moderate expenditures; (3) substitution of donations to worthy causes for gifts of flowers by friends and relatives; (4) holding of burial service shortly after
death or within two days; (5) holding the funeral in the church; (6)
appropriate dignified music; (7) elimination of procession to the
grave, or committal service for the family only.

The Middletown Association also advocated that the family decide on a fraternal order service or one by a clergyman and that Sunday funerals be eliminated. It maintained that respect for the dead
and "fine funerals" are not related. The ministers in Elgin recommended that the family and minister agree on time and place of the
memorial service before information is given to the press. They declared that reading of an obituary is unnecessary, and that any expression of appreciation of the minister's services should not go
through the undertaker's hands. Among the statements made by the
Oxford group are: (1) plans should be made with church and undertaker prior to death, (2) embalming usually is not necessary, (3)
"open house" at the funeral parlor should be discontinued, (4) bodies
might be designated for use by research laboratories, (5) cremation
should be available if desired, (6) covering of the casket in church
by a pall is desirable and (7) the entire service should be conducted
by the minister.

It can be seen that many of these proposals run counter to the interests of the funeral director. The practices of the undertakers
which these churches opposed are: emphasis on delay of burial and
on embalming and "restoration," showing the remains, display and

expensive ("fine") funerals, planning with the family and control from that time by undertakers, lavish floral exhibits, and extensive use of funeral parlors. That the projects initiated in Middletown, Elgin and Oxford carried only as far as they did, in the face of the support of the parishioners was ascribed by some of the participants to several causes. Among them was the matter of individualism and lack of unity among Protestant groups, as well as the reluctance to oppose any business interests. I would add the lack of attention generally given to death and funerals.

Chapter VII

THE UNDERTAKER'S ROLE IN THE COMMUNITY

... each man is preferred according to his virtue or to the esteem in which he is held for some special excellence.
                                                                    THUCYDIDES

The place the funeral director holds in the community affects in extraordinary degree the pressures he feels and the methods he uses in his business dealings. In indirect ways, but in very considerable measure, his status among the citizenry has helped to determine the character of modern funeral procedures. The obverse is certainly as true, perhaps even prior in importance: the business of the mortician affects his standing in the community, particularly the kind of social reaction accorded him. There are no caste lines, nor hard and fast rules of interaction between funeral directors and others; furthermore, any discrimination shown them varies greatly in different localities and circumstances. Hence the peculiarities of that unique observance, the funeral, are better understood if the major domo is put under scrutiny, not in any intimate, personal sense, but in respect to the main characteristics of the place he holds in his immediate society.

Aversion to Undertakers and Funeral Establishments. There exists a very distinct aversion to proximity to a lifeless body, especially that of a human being, an aversion that is very generally felt, although in differing degrees. It is quite obviously an impulsive reaction rather than a rational one. Historical accounts indicate clearly that it operated in previous generations among the family members whose duty it was to prepare the body of the deceased for burial. It made unpleasant in one particular, at least, the period in which the body lay in the home previous to the funeral. Observing the behavior of the survivors of a family diminished by death, and discussing with the members their feelings toward the body, leaves no doubt but that one of the foremost reasons the mortician's services are acceptable is the desire to turn the body over to him.

The aversion to the remains is not thereby eradicated, however; it is transferred in some measure to the person who has taken charge of them. The result is a strong tendency on the part of some persons to avoid contact with the undertaker, a general feeling of uneasiness in his presence, and a suppression or lack of such reaction on the part of a few. The injustice of the aversion is as great as its irrationality. But that it exists is not to be questioned; it is exhibited and admitted by the majority of persons.

The abhorrence of the remains, in conflict with the love of the person who has died, is, as has been indicated, a factor in the feeling of guilt that exaggerates the desire for expensive funerals. It leads to the curious and still more irrational desire for permanence of the body as it is, and consequently helps to sell metal caskets and supposedly indefinitely durable vaults to preserve the remains. The belief in the resurrection of the body has no logical relation to the desire to preserve it as it existed at death. In fact, at least for one group of persons believing in the resurrection of the body, the traditional hope exists that the elements of the body unite themselves rapidly with the earth in which the remains are laid.

The undertakers are very defensive on the subject of aversion to themselves. Frequently they deny that any such aversion to them exists at all. However, in discussion, almost any of them will expand on the injustice of such a reaction at much greater length than would be normal if no actual slight were felt. Nearly half the number interviewed told of experiences in which, because of their occupation, they were not as readily accepted as other persons. They speak of the persistent tendency of their acquaintances to joke about the undertaker's connection with dead bodies. There are individuals among them who put a reverse twist on their connection with death and utilize it to attract attention. For example, in at least two cities are firms, each of which presents to a thoroughfare a side of its building on which are painted the words: "Go slow; we can wait."

There are more evidences of the feeling of an aversion to undertakers in small towns than in cities, a fact probably due not so much to the greater modernization of the city, as to the closer relationship, actual or potential, of acquaintances in small communities. Also in the large establishments, found more frequently in the cities, the funeral director is not so closely identified with the actual handling of bodies as in the small, since embalmers are employed for the purpose. A larger proportion of clients are primarily customers, not personal friends. Funeral directors often express the opinion that aversion to association with them is dying out; that it is old fashioned and is gradually disappearing with the growth of appreciation of the difference between the "undertaker" of decades ago and the modern "funeral director." Conclusion from investigation runs counter to the statement, however. The undertaker of generations ago lived in a more closely knit community, and the contacts he made were more likely to overcome the aversion felt toward him than in the more casual relationships of today. Furthermore, until the advent of funeral parlors to which bodies were taken, families were in as much contact with their own dead during the period before burial as were the undertakers, since the bodies lay at home; and hence the undertaker was not in as much of a special relation to bodies. From the references in literature, from diary entries, and from the testimony of those old enough to recall the attitudes of two and three generations ago, there is no evidence that any considerable change has taken place in the attitudes toward dead bodies or toward undertakers.

Friendship overcomes aversion based on an initial feeling toward an undertaker's tasks; at least there are cases which prove that it often does. Presumably friendship is seldom formed when the repulsion has been too great in the first place. Cultural influences work to lessen or increase the acceptability of the funeral director. In different contexts he is "derisively accepted"; he is avoided; he is a leader in certain minority groups, with popularity that waxes or wanes according to his usefulness while the group is becoming assimilated into the culture of the new land.

Avoidance of close association with undertakers, even in situations in which it is hardly discernible, shows itself on occasion in many unexpected ways. The case of a very prominent leader in a large metropolitan community will serve to illustrate many that might be told. As chairman of a representative citizens' body, there was submitted to him a long list of prospective new members. He crossed off a prominent name solely on the basis of the individual's occupation— that of undertaker, saying that others would not feel so free to join the group if he belonged.

The funeral establishment possesses the same capacity to repel as the person of the funeral director. In fact, it is objected to much more frequently and overtly. Often, even when he is accepted apparently in every social or civil connection, the locating of his place of business in a residential area is resisted vigorously. Almost invariably the greatest, and often the sole objection is the nature of the business. The legal aspects of the issue are summarized in an article which appeared in the *American Funeral Director*: "an ultimate decision in favor of objecting neighboring property owners may rest upon one or both of two grounds: (1) That the municipal authorities have used reasonable judgment in zoning the district, (2) That the owners of adjacent property are entitled to enjoin the project if they can prove that it would constitute a nuisance to them." (1, p. 88)

In order to lessen the suspicion of the public and its aversion to the funeral parlor, leaders in the industry have advocated that representative persons be invited by the funeral directors to visit and inspect their plants. "It is time that the public is given the facts and taken into our confidence," writes one undertaker in the *American Funeral Director*. He advocates inviting whole groups at special hours as well as individuals: "There are two main reasons why this program is generally valuable. First, it enables a group of people who are not under any immediate emotional stress to get acquainted with the funeral director and his staff. Generally, these visitors find their hosts are 'just folks,' friendly and courteous and helpful. Also they get an idea of the special knowledge and skills that lie behind the staging of a funeral." (2, p. 23)

The author is referring to a problem that confronts the host on the tour of inspection: shall the preparation room be shown or "simply ignored." On this point there is sharp division of opinion among undertakers.

Ultra-Respectability of the Undertaker. The aversion to human remains that is projected on to the funeral director has a bearing on another aspect of his acceptance in the community, namely, the expectation that he will be well behaved according to a strict interpretation of the accepted norms. Without exception the funeral directors tell about it, although in about half the instances there is a conviction that the pressure on them is steadily lessening. In these cases there is agreement that in the larger towns the undertaker can afford to conduct himself much as the practitioners of other vocations do. Nevertheless there is a general recognition that in the matter of ultra-respectability, particularly as connected with sex morals and the consumption of liquor, the undertaker suffers constraint. Not only the funeral directors themselves, but the national associations and the embalming schools as well, stress the importance of good character and acceptable behavior of the practitioner.

An assumption sometimes made is that the expectation of greater regard for respectability on the part of funeral directors is due to the wish of the family of the deceased to avoid the possibility of mistreatment of the body of the loved person. Laws of several states requiring that a woman be in attendance when a female's remains are embalmed are of the same order. But this explanation falls short of adequacy. In the case of the Catholic and the Jewish groups there are strong religious reasons for the demand that the body, which is to figure in the future life, be treated only by trustworthy hands. And yet the pressure on funeral directors for a greater show of conformity is no stronger in these than in certain other groups.

There is reason to believe that the client requires more than the usual assurance of the moral and ethical acceptability of the funeral director in order to overcome his reluctance to join in mutual activity with him. To put it in another way, the community punishes the undertaker because of its own ambivalence toward him, in something like a scapegoat mechanism. He, in turn, accepts that phase of his role, because of his need to make friends in large numbers for business reasons, and also because his "impeccable character" has become a mark of status in the undertaking group. This explanation is strengthened by the fact that the advertising funeral directors, who rely more on commercial methods than on acquaintance and member-ships in organizations to attract patronage, cast off more completely the semblance or reality of ultra-respectability. The word "unctious," employed often by antagonistic critics to characterize the undertaker, is used by advertising undertakers occasionally to describe their non-advertising colleagues.

The funeral directors who operate in small towns, or within minor-ity groups in which friendly acceptance carries greater weight than in the less integrated urban communities, are cautious about any seeming lapse from strict observance of the rules of proper behavior. They say, for example, that they play cards at an intimate party but not at a bazaar; that they will drink beer at a social event among friends, but even then fear that a "call" may come and their drink-ing be revealed by the odor on the breath. Since funeral directors in small establishments may be called at any hour of the day or night, they run the risk of disapproval for any slight indulgence.

The generalization of the paragraph above holds good for a very large portion of the middle class families. A somewhat divergent attitude is to be found in some lower class families in which ultra-respectability is not prized so highly. Both clients and funeral di-rectors in communities composed largely of that group deny that undertakers are under any stricter need to act with rigorous propriety

than any one else. A family representative is likely to say he would
resent treatment from any one who is "stuck-up." Undertakers say
their customers like to be served by men who are sociable. Furthermore the rigidity of conduct between the undertaker and lady acquaintances does not hold. "The ladies like you to be gallant," or
words to that effect, is often said.

Type of Connection With Organizations. It has been said that
funeral directors have few friends, and since they join many organizations and societies to secure patronage, their social relationships
must be of a less friendly nature than those of individuals in other
callings. The argument goes on to suggest that the tendency to avoid
close association with these practitioners leads them to prefer the
casual, more formal and less personal associations that are found in
memberships to the closer relationship of friendship.

The argument is built largely on inference, and logical as it may
sound, I have not found it substantiated. The facts seem to amount
to the following. Many funeral directors complain earnestly that the
necessity to be on call constantly, as is true in the great majority of
firms, reduces drastically their opportunity to engage in social activities in any satisfying degree. The second consideration that affects
the depth of their relations to others is the very common practice of
joining many organizations and societies. In those societies they
make their appearances, many of them state, and do whatever pleas-
ing things they can while not spending much time in the process.
Generous purchasing at bazaars and "fairs" is often spoken of in this
connection.

One other argument has been advanced: that undertakers exert
themselves unduly to seem friendly to customers and in so doing they
lessen their own capacity for true friendship. It is true that they do
attempt zealously to act in friendly fashion, and frequently they
overshoot the mark. Nevertheless, no intelligent person could listen
to the saccharine commercials of almost any type of business over
the radio or television and adjudge the undertakers as worse. Time
for social experience is limited for them; they do spread their memberships thin; but the fact seems to be quite clear that they have
close friendships, prize them and would welcome the opportunity to
foster them more than they do.

Effect of the Funeral Business on Family Life. Among the undertakers in whose establishments each constitutes the only responsible
person who can deal with clients—and they comprise the great ma-

jority of all—there is agreement that the demands of the business reduce drastically the time that can be given to their families. Each is confined to the funeral home for many hours of the day, to be on hand if a call for service comes. Even when at home many feel the responsibility of remaining within reach when the telephone rings. The uncertainty of the day and hour when the next call will be received either prevents or makes very tentative any plans for social engagements outside the home or for entertaining in it.

In the larger firms in which the responsibility of office attendance can be allotted in part to competent associates, this problem is not encountered. The size of the firm in like manner governs the degree to which the nature of the undertaker's vocation affects the family of the funeral director. In general the proximity of the living quarters to the mortuary most vitally determines the effect of the business on the family. When the home is located in the same building, as occurs in the smallest establishments occasionally, the complaints mount highest.

A very human and entertaining, as well as authentic account of the burden of such an arrangement on the children, is to be found in a book written by the daughter of an undertaker of the old school. Although he was a highly admired and respected and greatly liked person, and although she experienced great pride in the father's place in the esteem and affections of the townspeople, she suffered shame nonetheless because of the taunts of her young companions. As she reached the age when the first suitor appeared, she came face to face with bitter frustration when he was discouraged at first by the coffins in the building and later by the presence there of the body of a customer. (3, pp. 99-106)

Experiences of this type cause some undertakers to separate home and place of business as widely as possible. One will tell of purchasing a home in a suburb, another of his son's determination after finishing law school, to set up a business in another city, in order to keep the knowledge of his father's occupation from prospective customers. His is an extreme case; normally disability of the kind described, felt by children of funeral directors, varies according to size of the town, integration of the ethnic or religious group, financial status of the firm and the geographical as well as social distance between the home and the business quarters.

Claim to Professional Status. A persistent drive to gain recognition as a profession is met everywhere among the leaders in the associations of funeral directors, in the trade periodicals, in the announcements of the mortuary schools, and among some of the successful proprietors of establishments. Even among the latter, however, there is nothing like agreement on the issue, and in the rank and file of undertakers few come out flatly and declare themselves professional. "We are business men" says the largest group; "of a professional kind but lower than doctors or lawyers," says a smaller group; "not yet, but advancing in that direction," still fewer reply. A large number decline to admit that the question is significant so far as they understand its relation to their vocational responsibilities. The funeral directors belonging to the advertising group with few exceptions declare undertaking is purely a business. One of them compared a hypothetical degree of "Doctor of Mortuary Science" to a "Doctor of Carpentry."

The claim to professionalism on the part of funeral directors has gone to extreme lengths and has resulted in occasional unforeseen developments. One is reported without comment in the *Southern Funeral Director*: "Grave digging is a service, not a profession, the Office of Price Stabilization ruled and the Lake View Cemetery Association at Fort Atkinson will have to roll back their prices. The decision came after the cemetery group raised prices recently and maintained the diggers were professional men." (4, p. 18)

One foundation on which the claim of professionalism has been based is the training for embalming—involving, as it does, a certain degree of knowledge of chemistry, anatomy, bacteriology, histology and pathology. One authority says: "I feel strongly that the only essence of professionalism in the industry lies in the work which the embalmer is required to do. It is the licensed embalmer who performs the necessary operations which are primarily for public health and welfare." (5, p. 38) However, embalmers in many establishments are members of trade unions, and as such classified often with workers. In addition the funeral directors who do not do their own embalming are prone to regard embalmers as skilled workers or technicians.

The provision for licensing alone justifies the argument in favor of professional recognition in the minds of a few undertakers. Association with representatives of professions and businesses, such as physicians, coroners, health officers and the clergy, reflects a bit of the color of the professional on him, it is maintained. Other undertakers emphasize the fact that they deal with individual cases; and say that therefore theirs is a personal service. The most enthusiastic claimants for professional standing recognize the distinction between business and professional activity, and for the most part content themselves by stating that undertaking involves both. Even the business administration of the funeral director has been advanced as a professional aspect of his activities. "Both merchandising and labor relations, so far as they are the abstract development of practices that have a material application," according to *Casket and Sunnyside,* "have come to assume something of the status of sciences, and thereby have a professional character." (6, p. 15)

In the state of New Jersey, ambition for recognition of embalmers and undertakers as professionals has climbed to the height of a legislative pronouncement. The first step toward that goal was representation in the New Jersey Council of Professional Societies. Later the following paragraph became a part of the "New Mortuary Science Act," quoted in the journal of the New Jersey State Funeral Directors Association: "In the interest of, and to better secure, the public health, safety and welfare, and for the more efficient administration and supervision of sanitary codes and health regulations, the practice of mortuary science and the practice of embalming and funeral directing are hereby declared to be a profession." (7, p. 4)

Turning to the question: why does the industry struggle to have itself looked upon as professional rather than as commercial, especially in a society in which commerce and industry are ascribed such high status, the answer is fairly evident. The effort is an integral part of the movement in the industry to elevate the funeral in the eyes of the public. Probably very little thought has been given by the majority of individuals in the trade to any significance in the term "professional," other than a higher status for the business and the practitioners in it. Some of the more lowly undertakers have frankly uttered suspicion that it is an effort of the successful individuals eventually to shut them out of the business, and to concentrate more of it in the hands of the few. A characterization of the effect on the part of several vocations to achieve professional status has been made by Everett Cherrington Hughes:

" . . . profession is not so much a descriptive term as one of value and prestige. . . . It happens over and over that the people who practice an occupation attempt to revise the conceptions which their various publics have of the occupation and of the people in it. In so doing, they also attempt to revise their own conceptions of themselves and of their work. The model which these occupations set before themselves is that of the 'profession.' . . . The movement to 'professionalize' an occupation is thus collective mobility of some among the people in an occupation. One aim of the movement is to rid the occupation of people who are not mobile enough to go along with the changes . . . it is common in our society for occupational groups to step their occupation up in the hierarchy by turning it into a profession." (8, p. 315)

Despite the boot-strap effort to become a profession, unanimous opinion prevails in the industry that it is primarily a business, no matter what else it is. The undertaker, according to this view, is a dual personality—on the one hand a well-trained professional man expertly preparing the body and ministering to the bereaved; on the other hand a highly efficient, practical business man who manages a complex funeral establishment, hires and directs employees, sells caskets and other merchandise, and handles collection problems. The professional aspect of the work of the funeral director, it is maintained, should be stressed for the purpose of achieving better public relations and of giving support to the individual proprietor in his negotiations with his clients: "But behind all of this professional atmosphere . . . there is and must be a business structure which should be maintained along modern, efficient lines . . . the public as a whole has not given full recognition to the value of our service. This public attitude, together with the fact that we sell merchandise as well as service, has materially complicated our problem. Instead of being able to obtain a proper fee for our services, old-established custom compels most of us to include the major portion of our service charges in the price of the casket." (9, p. 27)

The dual hope that undertaking will find a higher level in public opinion, and that the rise in status will result in greater ability to make a higher charge for services through a recognition of professional attitude and quality in the funeral director, was expressed clearly in an editorial in the *Southern Funeral Director*: "There is something of the 'professional' . . . a sincere desire to place a service above all other objectives . . . markedly apparent in those who are now engaged in funeral service. . . . We are not so naive as to believe that the art of embalming is a profession. . . . Neither do we accept the contention of some that the management . . . of a funeral service establishment is wholly professional . . . it is not the boot-strap self lifting occasionally proposed in legislative halls and elsewhere . . .

it is the over-all growth in stature of the whole funeral service personnel that we note. . . . S.F.D. hopes that funeral service will reach that degree of professionalism that will permit a professional service charge entirely independent of a merchandise charge. . . . When it arrives there will be an end to public, press, radio and other assertions that funeral service costs too much." (10, p. 6)

Reduced to its elements, the motivation of the funeral director's demand for professional standing would seem to consist of: (1) a desire to find validation for his belief that he is at liberty to charge for funerals prices that he regards as fair, and (2) egositic satisfaction the need for which is exaggerated by a realization of incomplete social acceptance.

Public opinion rates the funeral director below any group of professional workers, as revealed in the survey of the National Opinion Research Center in the spring of 1947. The undertaker received a score of 72. Scoring ahead of him were: welfare worker, 73; public school teacher, 78; biologist, 81; sociologist, 82; priest, 86; lawyer, 86; minister, 87; physician, 93. The highest score for any vocation was 96 for a United States Supreme Court Justice. Business occupations scoring above the undertaker were: owner and operator of a printing shop, 74; owner of a factory employing 100 people, 82; banker, 88. Below the undertaker were: manager of a store in a small city, 69; owner and operator of a lunch stand, 62. Among laborers, the undertaker scores between a trained machinist, 73 and a bookkeeper, 68, or a carpenter, 65. His score comes between a captain in the regular army, 80, and a corporal, 60.

The study made for the National Funeral Directors Association places the undertaker in a more favorable position. In it, 38 per cent of the respondents checked the statement that he is a professional man on the same level as the doctor or the lawyer, 33 per cent checked the statement that he is a professional man, but of lower status than doctor or lawyer; and 29 per cent checked the statement that he is a business man. (11, p. 25) The majority of the clergy queried on this point regarded the undertaker as a business man. Predominantly the clients whom I questioned classified him as a business man, with the status accorded a business man of approximately the same investment. It is clear from what has been said that the leading funeral directors have more assurance of their own professionalism than do others. A final word on their claim should be based on the analysis of professionalism offered by sociologists who have written most authoritatively on the subject.   (12, p. 284), (13, p. 476), (14, chs. VIII and IX)

The practice of law and medicine are regulated by the state, say Carr-Saunders and Wilson (12, p. 478), to distinguish competent practitioners for any member of the public who may require of them a vital or fiduciary service at a moment's notice.   The funeral director qualifies in this item although question might be raised as to the measure of faith the client can place in his advice.   For Parsons, authority in a professional field is based on technical competence in a defined area. Competence of the undertaker, as has been shown, is a very general ability.   The training that he undergoes is given in a year or less, and consists of acquiring elementary knowledge in subjects covered with much greater thoroughness in medical training.   The specific nature of competence is central to the whole concept of professionalism; and this specificity applies only to one relationship.   The doctor is given confidence and his orders are followed only in the area of his training and specific ability, namely, the illness because of which the patient has put himself under the direction of the expert.

At this point also the funeral director falls short of professional standards.   Not only is his expertness exceedingly limited despite his specializing in funerals, but specialization in funerals requires diffuse activities.   Further he claims competence, not in a limited, defined area in which he is highly trained, but in many fields in which he is not professionally trained at all.   His is not the interest of the doctor in that one aspect of his client, the illness, without regard to friendliness, neighborliness and common membership in social, civic and religious groups.   These latter do not enter the professional's relationship to his client.   They not only enter the relationship of undertaker and customer; they are sought after and emphasized by the former.

One striking illustration of the lack of professional attitude on the part of the funeral director is his common assertion that his chief service to the bereaved family is the solace he gives in their grief. It is the solace of a person untrained in the methods of assistance to individuals in situations of the kind.   There is in his mind no idea of narrowing his relations to the function in hand in order to perform that function professionally.   The function that he performs is not one of professional nature.   In the first place, as has been indicated, the activities of the few days or hours before burial or cremation, cannot, because of limitation of time, be more than routine and superficial.

In the second place, the whole context of the funeral, other than in its religious significance, does not provide for the development of relationships in which professionalism can operate. As Parsons has pointed out, a profession centered in one aspect only of the client's welfare, requires for its functioning a complex interrelationship with other parts of the social system. In the nature of the case, expertness in a specific field must relate itself to expertness in other fields, and to the institutions of society. Funeral operations are peculiarly unrelated, or related very casually to the functioning of other segments of society. The funeral is in a context of its own; the funeral director is, in the most significant aspects of his vocation, a law unto himself.

Because of that fact the funeral director has less of a sense of obligation than is to be found in professions; he feels himself only vaguely identified with the rules of the game that are so much of the pattern of professional behavior. It is because of the lack of a specific, limited and defined field within which he is authoritatively trained and oriented, that he must strive for professional status through self assertion rather than specific accomplishment of high order. He has no standards by which to show professional achievement except generalities which do not apply.

Funeral directing is not a profession.

Community Leadership by Funeral Directors. Assertions are very frequently made about the relatively large numbers of undertakers who allegedly become prominent leaders, especially in the realm of politics. Investigation reveals scattered cases of modest leadership responsibility, but no more than would fall to the lot of almost any vocational group of like size. The ratio of leaders to the total number in the group falls below the ratio to be found among lawyers. For the most part the funeral directors themselves react to a query regarding the matter with statements that there is no undue number of them in prominent civic or public office and there is no reason why the number should be brought into question. They refer in speeches and print to funeral directors as prominent citizens, meaning usually that they participate in many organized activities.

Many of the persons who raise the issue of community leadership by undertakers, at the same time question the propriety of it, or suggest that some suspicion attaches to it. Apparently three assumptions account for the attitude of those who hold this point of view. First, there is a vague and seldom expressed impression that the undertaker who functions in the realm of death and funerals is not a part of the workaday world; that he does not fit there. Second, the aversion entertained toward him expresses itself in suspicion of leadership by him. Third, the political leader is regarded by some as a manipulator; the funeral director is looked on in something of the same light and a combination in one person's activities of politics and undertaking makes him doubly suspicious.

In point of fact, the cases in which funeral directors are leaders of some consequence require no explanation other than the circumstances in which they occur. For one thing, small towns may present instances of combination of civic and undertaking responsibility, along with other combinations of activities. Funeral directing and furniture or other business is also found under one roof in the smaller cities and towns.

Another context in which leadership often falls to the lot of the undertaker, again is due to the circumstances of the group he serves more than to the peculiarities of his vocation. It is the immigrant group in its earliest stages of assimilation. The undertaker is one of the few who meet public officials, and even in a limited way, "knows his way around." He can read and write and not infrequently he is a notary public. Occasionally he becomes a leading figure, representing the whole group in dealings with local politicians and others. At a later stage of assimilation, the immigrant lawyer seems to have more chance of becoming leader. It is the stage when members of the group may own property or run small stores.

In large cities, except among immigrant peoples, undertaking and large leadership responsibility do not go together except in rare instances. When they do combine they have seemed to separate eventually. The most successful individuals working in two fields, one of which is undertaking, tend to give up one or the other. Particularly from the few undertakers who have also been politicians, the explanation given for the relinquishment of one field is that, while political prominence may add to the acquaintances of the funeral director, it also tends to limit actual clientele to the members of one political party. The trade journals carry articles occasionally advising participation in civic activities and attendance at church, but warning that positions of leadership in these fields may result in making some enemies. Political activities are regarded as fraught with danger for the business.

Outside the small town and immigrant groups exceptional circumstances can be found when funeral directors in large numbers become politicians. One such situation prevailed in a large city in which five out of eighty funeral directors were also politicians; three of them were holding public city office in the middle range of importance. The factors in the situation which explain the unusual incidence of combined undertaking and public office include the following. First, a mortuary school is located in the city and it has been well attended. In consequence, there is in the city more than the usual ratio of funeral directors to the total population, and their establishments attract customers in numbers inadequate to furnish a good living. Second, the funeral directors do not advertise, with the exception of the one representative of the advertising group in the city. It is conceivable that the prohibition of all kinds of advertising (even in the telephone book) tends to force extraordinary use of other methods of contacting families. Third, there is an unusual proportion of funeral directors combining other types of work with their undertaking, including skilled labor and business.

On the basis of the evidence it is reasonable to conclude that funeral directors do not become political leaders in undue numbers. As a matter of general observation it can confidently be said that as a group they influence community affairs very little, particularly when they are compared to the clergy, lawyers, professors or physicians.

Funeral Directing as a Career. Since the mortician is subject to the demands of an exacting vocation on him and his family, and since the community does not offer large honorific reward for his labors, it becomes a matter of more than usual interest to see what his career does give him, what the inducements are to enter it, and what sort of satisfactions he gets from it. It is well to look into his individual role as a proprietor in an unusual business before dealing with the business as a whole and its part in shaping the form and conduct of funerals in the United States.

The choice of undertaking as a calling is determined for the individual by circumstance oftener than by unfettered selection from a variety of possibilities, especially by the circumstances of family connection with the business. It is the father-to-son succession that induces many to enter it. When the father does not transmit the business, then the influence of some other relative, by blood or by

marriage, usually provides the suggestion or the opportunity to get
started. In not a few instances the inducement is more than an opportunity, it is a family duty to continue an established enterprise
that may not be so attractive as some other calling. It is also a second choice for some individuals frustrated in a desire to go into medicine, the law, or even professional baseball. On the whole, however,
undertaking offers an opportunity willingly embraced. Especially is
this true in the case of those who come into the work from a related
field, such as the livery business which has furnished the original
family connection for at least a number of funeral firms.

Recruiting appeals, which indicate the incentives that probably
lead to the choice of vocation, stress economic security and inde-
pendence. The large associations and the mortuary schools in their
recruitment pamphlets warn that expectancy of great financial returns is liable to frustration. The drawbacks are seldom minimized
in these appeals.

There is no one type of person who enjoys and succeeds in undertaking, to be sure; but there is fairly general agreement among practitioners, leaders in the associations and directors of mortuary schools
on the question of personal characteristics that best fit individuals
for the work. First is desire and ability to work with people, second
is conformity to the norms of respectability in the community. It
is often labelled "good habits" and "strength of character," although
the latter also means ability to stick out the periods of difficulty.
Willingness to give service, especially to join organizations, is promi-
nently mentioned, and also ability to work hard and continuously.
There are women practitioners and successful ones, sometimes widows
of funeral directors. Men predominate, however.

To become a manager is a long and difficult road to travel if one
starts from the bottom. The only easy way is to inherit the business
or to buy into it, opportunities obviously not open to many aspirants.
Apprenticeship for a year, and attendance at mortuary school for the
same length of time or the greater part of it, are the first two hurdles.
In the larger establishments advancement may lie through periods of
service as licensed embalmer, assistant funeral director, or branch
manager. Because of the slow rate of mobility and the exactions of
the work a considerable proportion of those who enter it without
the benefit of family connection do not remain. To the question,
asked in a study made by leaders in the trade, "If you were to again
choose a vocation would you choose the same as you did?", 40 per

cent replied in the negative, 31 per cent that they were uncertain. The perennial shortage of applicants to fill the personnel needs of the trade, especially in years of full employment, leads to advocacy by leading writers of: better working hours and conditions for employees in funeral homes, leniency by state licensing boards, and occasionally to a suggestion of a moratorium on advance in educational requirements for applicants.

Despite the negative aspects of the business there is great stability to be observed, especially if change in ownership and direction is compared with change in other lines of business. The proprietors stick to their tasks. In return they get modest economic security for the application of prolonged effort, great industry, and the sacrifices of many hours each day. It is not the field for great adventure, nor for quick returns and large reward for small effort. It offers satisfactions to men and their families who are content to work in a stable occupation over long periods of time. For the majority of proprietors, there have been no tragic disappointments; they were aware of the lack of great money making possibilities from the time of their first commitments. Many would like to achieve greater financial success than has been possible, particularly in view of the large sums accumulated by a very few of their colleagues.

However, hope for pecuniary success is limited among funeral directors by the realization of lines of stratification. The large or "volume" establishments require correspondingly large investments not within the reach of the great majority. Social and ethnic lines are drawn more tightly than in many lines of economic enterprise. The minority group undertaker serves his group for the most part. The manager of a dingy parlor in a lower class neighborhood has little opportunity to make large profit. So, too, the funeral home that for generations has served "the best families" is not to be compared in the matter of possible economic returns with the run of the mill establishment. There is much feeling of class and group identification on the part of the funeral directors. It furnishes a basis of satisfaction for those who have served a clientele of distinction or high social class.

Undertakers who have felt themselves identified for many years with the calling often express a sense of satisfaction at having persisted in a difficult task. Many of them feel that they have been "kicked around," but take pride in having done what they consider an essential service in the community. They say they have helped people and have been shown gratitude by some of their clients. Pride is not at all uncommon among them in the artistry of restoration of faces and in the long succession of "fine funerals," each of which made noteworthy occasions, they think, in the lives of many acquaintances and friends. Lastly the great majority of them take satisfaction in having maintained the funeral home for years or decades.

In these men, then, in the many communities in the country, there is a group of respectable, stable individuals, identified closely with family establishments over long periods of time, expecting no windfalls of large amounts of money, putting in long hours, forced to watch for every possibility of meeting the expenses of running their institutions and making a modest living. For organizational purposes they would seem to provide good material for the leaders who could unify them around a common interest.

CHAPTER VIII

DOMINANCE OF COMMERCIAL FACTORS

Commerce defies every wind, outrides
every tempest, and invades every zone.
INSCRIPTION OF A BROOKLYN BANK

The funeral director is not vitally influenced by any of the groups in the community. Nevertheless he and his competitors act similarly in many ways. These two facts lead to a supposition that there must be some sort of group or organization which serves as a guide to him, and from which he derives inspiration and moral support. Funeral establishments reveal a high degree of similarity in equipment, operation and goods and services offered. Beliefs, attitudes and ideals of undertakers are strikingly alike. Their pattern of thought and action must be formed in some common matrix.

The source of uniformity in the practices and convictions of undertakers is to be found in the leadership given to the business by city, state, and national trade associations. The organized expressions of the business needs of undertaking are coordinated in a national grouping, and the needs of all establishments are determined largely on a national scale. As a result the patterns of the undertaking business are formed primarily on a country-wide basis. The funeral director, responding to the picture of the needs of the total industry presented by the leaders in the associations, finds himself, therefore, still more insulated from local community influences.

National Scope of Business Pressures. The nation is greatly overstocked with funeral establishments. In order to survive funeral directors adopt devices to raise prices and maintain them at a high level, since reliance on increasing volume of trade is precluded. In a study of this problem in 1950 the National Funeral Directors Association received 10,348 replies to a questionnaire sent to a carefully compiled list. A report of that survey includes the following statement: "The total number of funeral homes in the United States at the present time is 23,827. The population of the United States, according to the last reports we had, which is unofficial, is approximately

147 million people. This means—that there is one funeral home for every 6,181 persons. For the same year there were 1,376,083 deaths. This means—there are only 57 deaths per year per funeral home in the United States." (1)

The significance of these figures becomes more evident when it is seen how large a proportion of the firms get less than the average number of funerals per year. A survey made among representative mortuaries in 1945 indicated the number of adult funeral services conducted each year by individual funeral homes as follows:

Annual Services per Firm	*Per Cent of Firms*
Less than 50 adult services	43%
50-100 adult services	32%
100-175 adult services	16%
More than 175 adult services	9%

(This data does not include children, embalming only, or services on funerals received from out of town for local burial.) (2, p. 12).

The Managing Director of National Selected Morticians, Inc., emphasizes the over-abundance of funeral establishments and the struggle for survival that the lesser firms go through: "There are too many firms in this business. . . . 2000 firms could do all the business in America. There are now over 20,000. In a mid-western town of 120,000 population there are 7 establishments; 2 of them do 85% of the business. The others of necessity are small. In a town of 80,000 population 4 firms exist, each with a complete establishment. One of the firms takes 45% of the business; a second takes 35%; the other two divide the remainder." (3)

The number of deaths in the country remains approximately the same from year to year, and the funeral business, therefore, finds little chance for expansion from that source. From 1940 to 1952 the number of deaths varied only from 1,417,269 to 1,496,838, a rise of less than 6 per cent. Meanwhile the mortality rate itself declined from 10.8 per cent to 9.6 per cent. (4, p. XXIX)

Because of the basic importance for this study of the relation of the number of funeral firms to their success, a statistical demonstration of that relation is given. One starts with the assumption that the average receipts of the firms in an area can be correlated with the average population to be served by one firm in that area. Taking figures from the 1948 Census of Business, (5, p. 437) computation was made by the method of rank correlation for one hundred thirty cities of all sizes, selected at random from each state in the Union, in order to find a statistical figure which would serve as a measure of the correlation. That figure, the coefficient of correlation, was found to be high, namely, .66. If figures relating to only one section of the country had been used, the correlation would have been even more clearly demonstrated.

In a situation of this kind, at least three solutions, or partial solutions, would suggest themselves. The one which has been pressed throughout the industry most vigorously, and with no internal opposition, is to make funerals much more lavish and pretentious, thereby furnishing, in the higher prices asked, a basis for greater profits in each case. A solution of this kind allows the great majority of firms to stay in business. The second possible solution is to raise the standards of selection and training of undertakers and embalmers. This device has been used primarily to elevate the level of the whole industry, and thus to give better service and to justify funeral charges regarded as adequate. Inevitably the success it attains puts the more poorly trained proprietors at a disadvantage, and eliminates their competition.

The third device, approved throughout the industry, is the improvement of business methods. If pressed vigorously, particularly by the directors of the National Selected Morticians, for intensive self improvement, this results in the development of a number of successful firms using the best known competitive methods. The incidental result over a period of years would be the concentration of a larger amount of the total business in the hands of the abler directors and the eventual elimination of marginal establishments.

Rates of profit of firms of varying in size and efficiency are not available. According to Wilber M. Krieger, Managing Director of National Selected Morticians, Inc., whose experience is largely with the more successful enterprises, "a well-managed, well-operated funeral institution that is serving its community—which we believe is typical—will make 10 to 11 per cent profit. That's before taxes. . . . I could give you dozens and dozens of illustrations taken from studies of specific firms and prove that point in every size of funeral service business." (6, p. 41)

The annual receipts of funeral firms could provide a rough gauge of the success attained. However, average figures computed from U.S. Census Bureau returns constitute the only accessible information on that score. For the country at large the average receipts per establishment were $30,648 in 1948, and in that year the averages per establishment varied by regions from $26,363 in east south central area to $53,499 in the Pacific area. Average receipts per establishment by size of cities rose from the lowest, $21,094, for cities of 2500 to 4999 population, to $56,256 for cities of 250,000 to 499,999. Communities under 2500 population showed average receipts somewhat above those of the category immediately above them in population size; and cities of over 500,000 population showed average receipts per establishment somewhat lower than those in the 250,000-499,999 category. (5, p. 4, 17)

From the figures cited above it is readily seen that the funeral industry is in the category of small business. If the rate of 10 to 11 per cent profit, stated by Krieger holds good generally, the funeral business on an average gives small returns. For most of the funeral establishments the average rate is undoubtedly smaller. The solidarity of purpose, attitude, and method among the morticians is due to the fact that they are all in the same economic predicament and need to hang together in their dealings with customers and the public, in order to survive. A contributing factor which adds encouragement to their belief in "fine funerals" is the tacit alliance between them and the firms which supply them with goods. For these, too, hold a stake in the continuance of a high level of prices for the funeral in all its aspects. The Census of Manufactures of 1947 lists the value of mortician's goods "shipped" as $188,829,000. These include the products of establishments primarily engaged in manufacturing caskets, cases, supplies and accessories such as burial garments, gloves, slippers, casket linings, embalming fluids and mortician's paraphernalia and equipment. (7, p. 816)

In trade circles there are over 700 casket manufacturers known, over 100 firms dealing with embalming fluids, 75 concerns which make burial garments only. In one edition of the *American Funeral Director* there are advertisements of the following types each given here with the number of firms advertising in that one edition: 9 selling fluids; 2 partitions; 10 caskets; 13 mortuary schools; 3 lights; 21 accessories for caskets; 1 ornamental iron, 12 equipment; 2 floral racks; 6 musical records; 2 flowers; 8 vaults; 13 chairs and furniture; 1 air conditioning apparatus; 1 clothes for undertaker or the dead; 1 massaging vibrator; 12 motor cars; 5 cards and mementos; 2 books;

2 casket sealing material; 2 cosmetics; 1 grave tents; 1 fans; 2 crucifixes; 1 pins; and 1 sirens.

One organization represents funeral directors, cemetery officials, monument builders, concrete burial vault manufacturers, and florists. This is the Allied Memorial Council of Indiana, whose purpose is to promote better understanding of mutual problems and to oppose misrepresentation in the sale of their merchandise or services. In an editorial in *Casket and Sunnyside* the statement was made that "There are many known cases where funeral directors have gone into allied fields in a way to create ill feeling on the part of those whose interests are involved."

Public controversy with outside groups arises occasionally over the question of the wisdom, from the standpoint of the nation as a whole, of the amount of expenditures made for funerals. A notable one occurred in 1944, a brief account of which may serve to bring out the issues involved and the convictions of the leaders in the trade and their opponents. In an issue of *Newsweek* some of the material published previously, in the *Information Service* bulletin of the (then) Federal Council of Churches in America was quoted. The two were answered in an editorial in the *American Funeral Director*. Taking its figures from the *Survey of Current Business*, published by the U.S. Department of Commerce in 1944, the Federal Council of Churches bulletin editor estimated that in 1942 the public spent a total of $560,900,000 for funeral service, cemetery and crematory costs, monuments and tombstones. He compared this sum with the $720,800,000 spent in gifts and bequests during the same year to all organized religions; and the $578,300,000 for tuition at private schools and colleges and universities. However, the editor of the *American Funeral Director* saw no great significance in the figures cited (nor in data showing, as he pointed out, that $2,420,000,000 was spent for tobacco products, $618,500,000 for jewelry, and $404,800,000 for beauty parlor services, etc.) (8, p. 27) His position was as logical as that of the church editor, each was expressing his own set of values. Others at the time pointed up the issue more sharply by noting that the $618,500,000 spent for jewelry served a population of over 131,000,000 individuals for the whole year; whereas the $600,000,000 or less for funerals served for three days the immediate families of only one and one-half million who died. Presumably the reply to that statement would have been that to hold a fine funeral was worth all it cost because of the immediate pleasure it gave to the bereaved and the memories it made fresh for years afterward. It is at this point that the issue is joined, the one group maintaining that elaborate funerals give more satisfaction, the other maintaining that love and respect are better expressed in simpler burial and more emphasis on intangible values.

Adaptability of the Funeral Business. However solidly the under-taking group and its allies may hold together on policy and vocational procedure, the forms which the individual establishments take are di-verse in certain respects, and allow for adaptation to various forces and conditions. The Census of Business reported that 65 per cent of the establishments throughout the country are proprietorships, in which one man, or one man and his helper, usually perform all the services, perhaps with the part-time aid of a member of the proprie-tor's family. Twenty-three per cent are reported to be partnerships, and 12 per cent are corporations. In the last named the funeral di-rector is able to raise larger amounts of capital and is surer of a long-lived business, because the corporation remains in operation beyond the time of the death of any one owner. In the south and west the establishments take on the form of proprietorships in much smaller proportion. In the west partnerships are the largest category.

The business of undertaking fits into various sizes and degrees of completeness of establishments: (1) the single unit, complete type, equipped to handle all details connected with funeral service; (2) the multiple establishment in which a firm conducts more than one form of business, furniture, hardware, etc. as well as funeral direct-ing; and (3) the "broker" or "curb stone" type of funeral director who operates with little or no equipment and no building. He con-stitutes 5 per cent or less of all funeral directors and is blamed for many of the evils of the business by his colleagues in other categories. He is essentially a middleman, taking clients to the salesrooms of a casket maker, there to choose caskets, and having embalming done by a "trade" embalmer. It is apparent that he has little at stake so far as investment goes, and without a building he has less chance of securing patronage. Because of these two circumstances he is said to be more inclined to exploit customers when he does get them. Some of the leaders in the industry feel that curb stone operators are de-clining in number, because the majority of the public will not go along with an individual owning less than the minimum type of oper-ation.

About 10 per cent of funeral homes have branches. In this fashion the industry has adapted itself to the migration to the suburbs. As some of their clients move they are followed by the establishment of a branch in what is usually an area more promising for funeral business. Suburbs also offer one of the most promising areas to new establishments. There are a few chains of funeral homes, especially in New York City and Southern California. In California also can be found the colossal concern, owning many acres of burial ground for bodies or urns containing ashes, marble buildings housing columbaria and elaborate equipment, and controlling a multiple staff which furnishes funeral directing, cemetery or cremation services. Very few of these exist throughout the country and in some states a combination of these businesses is prohibited by law. In *The Loved One* Evelyn Waugh has described the "super-colossal" combination establishment of the Hollywood type, with its affected jargon, super salesmanship, and dripping sentimentality.

Mergers take their course in undertaking as in other business. They occur in cities and towns, especially when competing firms combine, and the two proprietors become partners. Mergers of large firms take place but are not so obvious to the public.

Funeral enterprise adapts itself to the distinctions of race and national origin. Immigrant peoples patronize funeral directors of their own ethnic origin for the first generation and in lesser measure in the second and third. Negro funeral directors are designated as such in the national directory of funeral establishments in order that the fact may be known when bodies are shipped from one city to another for burial. In mixed neighborhoods of Negroes and whites funeral directors of either group sometimes conduct funerals for one or the other, or for racially mixed clientele. In small towns, where there are apt to be no colored practitioners, white undertakers service them, without protest from or loss of other customers.

A firm serving largely a French clientele, may conduct comparatively simple funerals, since in France funerals are simpler than in America. On the other hand, Italians, who have seen elaborate funerals in Italy, soon after coming to the United States may utilize the funeral as an occasion for an elaborate gathering and a costly showing.

Adaptation as a characteristic of undertaking is seen in the way buildings of various types are used, from the store front in commercial zones of cities to the imposing fashionable structures in newly developed residential areas. The physical structure for funeral purposes has evolved with the development of technical and transportation facilities and with the increase in size of investment by the larger firms. The original store front form is found in the east more numerously; the converted, old, large and sometimes elegant homes are found in the middle west, where the initial buildings were often located in areas less densely populated. To erect structures specifically for funeral purposes was also more feasible at first in the west and later in the far west.

Leadership and Organization Structure. Certain economic factors in the United States produced a climate of opinion that has had something to do with the evolution of the lavish funeral. Families have had money to spend in increasing amounts and funerals have syphoned off part of it. Technology and mass production provided surprising and engaging gadgets to capture and hold popular attention. Along with these developments, secularism proceeded steadily despite growth in church membership. Materialism, however difficult to assess in its effects, has been one result of widespread consequence.

These factors played their part in the upward swing of the costs of burial and cremation. They are quite inadequate, however, to account completely for what took place. The specific ways these forces operated can be explained only with due allowance for the factor of manipulation of purchasing in the funeral context. The body is the most important material aspect of the funeral and a larger emphasis on it is to be expected in a materialistic age. That the emphasis should rest on sumptuous encasing of the dead body, to be buried in a few hours, was not an inevitable development, however. There well might have been costly memorials in the form of statues of the dead, or other more elaborate, costly, and spectacular forms than presenting a "restored" but a very fleeting object of attention. Ostentation and conspicuous consumption might have taken the form of ecclesiastical display, following the growth in church membership. After-burial parties might have devoured the surplus, if the caterers had had the inside track when death came to a family.

However, the funeral directors decreed otherwise. For them an overall strategy was essential for the long range needs of the funeral service group. A central authority was also needed to meet the need for day by day tactics. The United States spreads over a great deal of territory, and despite the uniformities of consumption within it, still contains cultural diversities of considerable magnitude and differing value systems subscribed to by various groups. Despite the fact that other organizations might have had a large stake in outlays for funerals, the profit to be made from them has been taken by the funeral directors, the cemeteries and the allied groups which supply them with materials. The accomplishment is to be credited largely to leadership that arose at the strategic moment.

Not only can it be said that leadership emerged, but leadership of a rather specific nature. Since there were no large sums of money, in comparison with the sums that often reward the entrepreneur in certain other lines of business in this country, the leadership could not be wholly like the usual risk taking individual in other commercial enterprises. Since the undertaking practitioners are scattered throughout the country, and are highly competitive, the leaders needed to develop an organizational structure to channel communication to the individual establishments. The benefits of organization had to be available to all practitioners. Lastly the objectives were not comprehensive enough, nor were they thought of as of sufficient concern to the welfare or idealism of communities, to inspire the loyalties of broad-gauged leaders. The idealism, the sanctity, the depth of feeling and the expression of permanent values were (and had been for generations) found in the religious aspect of funerals. In the light of the situation out of which funeral directing organizations grew, the accomplishments of the leaders have been remarkable.

The commercial influences on the funeral cannot be fully appreciated without knowledge of the organizational structures through which the leaders operate and the assumptions and ideology they express. The principal feature of that organizational structure, the National Funeral Directors Association, is a federation of state and local associations representing a large part of the vocation. Forty-seven states and the District of Columbia are represented. Only the New Jersey Association remains independent, and it is represented in the national organization by a considerable "at large" membership. The National Association has over 12,500 members. Assets in 1955 amounted to over $229,000, receipts to more than $164,000. Dues are paid by each establishment through its state association and constitute the bulk of the income of the Association. Its activities include educational services, working with the state associations and holding an annual convention and with it extensive exhibits. It makes studies, or has them made, and publishes bulletins. Among its chief interests are public relations and national and state legislation, especially government action relating to burial of members of the armed services, burial allowances to veterans, and relating to the beneficiaries of social security and public assistance.

The National Selected Morticians is formed on the Rotary Club plan whereby only selected firms meeting certain requirements of investment, establishment, equipment, sponsorship, and reputation, are taken into membership. It is a service organization for its approximately six hundred member firms in thirty or more states. For the services it renders directly to members on matters of business management it is able to assess dues of as much as $300. A majority of its members also belong to the National Funeral Directors Association. Closely related to it is the National Foundation of Funeral Service, a tax-exempt, educational institution housing the most adequate library of funeral service literature in the country. The related School of Management gives advanced courses designed primarily to secure better business efficiency and a larger volume of patronage for its membership firms.

Negroes belong to neither organization although there is collaboration between each of the two and the third grouping, the National Negro Funeral Directors Association. It has affiliates in twenty-four states and the Virgin Islands. The need for a separate association for Negroes, the white associations maintain, lies in the fact that while Negroes would be welcome, white representatives do not propose them as members, and hotels at which conventions are held will not give them room accommodations. It is also said that Negro undertakers face certain problems different from those of the white firms, such as the need to keep prices down in order to have greater assurance that the bills will be paid. (Colored funeral directors did not confirm this latter point in interviews.) Because of these difficulties and problems peculiar to Negro firms the white association leaders feel that separate groupings bring greater results. The Negro association follows many of the purposes of the N.F.D.A. including: better education and advocacy of higher standards for admission to the mortuary schools, state legislation, and participation of its members in government departments having to do with undertakers. Allied groups are local mortuary fraternities and a national women's auxiliary.

The Jewish Funeral Directors Association of America has slightly more than 150 members, almost all of whom belong to the National Funeral Directors Association. Orthodox, Conservative, and Reformed Jews belong to it. It deals with techniques of business management as well as with the conduct of funerals. The officers feel that it is not a separatist organization; that it exists to deal with problems unique in Jewish funerals. There is at least one problem it faces that is not a problem to the other national groups—namely, the orthodox Jewish funeral which is simple and inexpensive. The Hevrah Kadisha, the funeral society, which exists in some communities, is a feature also unique in Jewish funerals. In the remaining features of its activities it is not unlike the other national groups.

The National Advertising Funeral Directors Association is a group of 50 or more aggressive undertakers who are often criticized by the more conventional groups. They rely more on advertising to attract clientele and some of them disregard certain of the forms of "dignity" that characterize the ideals of the majority in the business. Some of the members are among the most financially successful of all funeral directors. One difference that has arisen between the Advertising and the other funeral directors' associations is the practice of advertising funerals at a given, minimum price, called "price advertising," a practice regarded as unethical by the majority of funeral directors. The crux of the difference seems to lie mainly in the attitudes of the two groups toward competition. Certain individuals in the Advertising Association say that the object of "price advertising" is to offer a competitive price, and not to engage in "bait advertising," and not merely to state the lowest price. Advertising is frowned on less now than formerly among funeral directors as a whole.

The members of the Advertising Association are scattered, appearing mostly in California, Colorado, New York, Pennsylvania, Illinois, Michigan, Texas, Utah, Massachusetts and the District of Columbia. The policy has been to have not more than one member in a locality, but also to develop chain operations, as has been done successfully in several cities, including Washington, Los Angeles and Syracuse.

There are a number of service organizations, such as: Associated Funeral Directors Service with approximately 1500 members, organized to stabilize service and charges on shipping cases; Federated Funeral Directors, which provides intensive bookkeeping service; and the American Funeral Directors Association, dealing with the subject of equipment.

Intercommunication in the field of funeral service takes place partly through the trade journals, conducted on independent business organization lines. The chief journal is the *American Funeral Director*, intimately to be identified with the policies of the National Funeral Directors Association. The bulletin and publications of the National Selected Morticians reach only the members. *Casket and Sunnyside*, a consolidation of earlier journals one of them first published in 1871, is the second most popular periodical. There are a number of regional journals, among them the *Southern Funeral Director*. In varying measure they bring together news of the National Funeral Directors Association, the National Selected Morticians, to less extent views of the other associations, the happenings in mortuary schools, developments of note in prominent establishments, and articles of general interest to funeral directors. They differ between themselves in emphases, but seldom come to a clash of opinion.

The picture of the whole organizational apparatus of the funeral business and the organs of communication, as they have been described above, appears somewhat splintered in form. The individual national associations represent only facets of a core of conviction and practices common to all of them. The National Funeral Directors Association represents the efforts to advance the industry as a whole. The National Selected Morticians and the National Advertising Funeral Directors Association represent, more specifically, the establishments which emphasize volume of trade as the chief desideratum, and therefore emphasize competitive business methods more and the neighborhood aspects of the funeral home less. The Negro and the Jewish Associations represent cultural differences.

Assumptions, Internal Discipline and Ideology. There is a striking similarity in the main assumptions, defenses, and strategy found in every part of the field. The associations, through member bulletins, meetings, reports, and the trade journals, transmit the thinking of the leaders to the funeral personnel, and to the public at large.

Reduced to their essential elements, what are the basic assumptions which ramify through the total structure? They are six in number: (1) the sentiment of the bereaved centers, or should center, around the dead body; (2) the expenditure for the funeral, up to the utmost capacity of the family to pay, is the one greatest criterion of the affection in which the dead was held; (3) the expenditure to be observed in the elegance of display at the funeral is a gauge showing the status of the dead and his family in the community; (4) the moral obligation rests on families to reveal their status through the style in which the funeral is conducted; (5) the beauty that is displayed at a funeral is a feature of the modern funeral. (This last assumption seems to be stated, not so much as implying a rule to be followed, as a fact that justifies the elaboration of funeral procedure in recent decades.) (6) The sixth assumption is seldom expressed in clearcut terms, especially as it applies to a specific funeral. The burden of it is that, apart from the religious aspects of funerals embodied in the rituals of certain faiths, a great social significance attaches to the disposal of the dead. This assumption goes beyond the sanitary factors involved. The statement that a nation is to be judged according to the manner in which it disposes of its dead, contains the idea. The use of the expression "the American way of burial" implies that anything short or different from, current practice would be a national disgrace.

These assumptions become, not just laws by which to judge action at funerals, but generalizations for all occasions and the total populace. Thus in the minds of undertakers the number and cost of floral pieces to be seen generally at funerals, come to be a measure of the amount of sentiment in the population. Curiously enough to an outsider, a report may be made to a funeral directors' convention that a trend back to sentiment can be seen in the country, when the fact the speaker has in mind is merely that more money is being spent on flowers for funerals than heretofore. Stemming partly from the doctrine of sentiment, and partly from the effort to demonstrate their professionalism, is the ethereal sounding jargon the associations are formulating and trying to inject into the English language. It is no longer "corpse" or "body," but "Mr. Smith," not "morgue" but "slumber-room," etc., etc. Official bulletins rejoicingly print the fact that another state convention has adopted the word "cremains" for "cremated remains." "We are informed," states a short article of 1948, "that this word has since been used in the *Reader's Digest!*"

The nation's intellectuals come in for their full share of resentment from undertakers, largely because among them is the greatest proportion of persons who do not accept the standard version of a "nice funeral." The criticism is voiced more often with direct or indirect reference to the intellectuals' failure to express sentiment in the fashion approved by funeral directors. The director of one of the most prominent national associations said, "Intellectuals don't have the same attitude as others. They like cremations. They are not interested in the body." The director of another association said, referring to intellectuals: "They should be told to be more human, to let the poor have the chance to express their love in fine funerals."

This is not the place to assess the validity of the assumptions made by the funeral trade. It is sufficient to point out here that: (1) sentiment of the deepest kind and of the greatest degree may not center on the dead body, and that it should be dissociated from it as rapidly as possible; (2) affection for the deceased is not necessarily related to the display at the funeral; there is no need at all for a public show of affection, and if there were, there are numerous socially beneficial ways of doing so; (3) even the funeral directors do not in practice observe a rule of regulating the costliness or display at funerals by the status of the family. They very frequently advise funerals on a level above that of the family's standing, and logically there is every reason to judge a family's place according to its accomplishments, not according to a sum spent at one critical juncture.

Further, it may be pointed out that: (4) there is no obligation on a family to proclaim its status; status is ascribed by others; (5) beauty is a matter of one's point of view and the prevailing aesthetic norms; and (6) while it is true that national ideals involve strict observance of the right of each religious group to follow its ritualistic procedures, and individual ideals should always include the utmost respect for the sanctities of others, it is also according to the heritage of this country that manner of disposal of its dead lies in the discretion of the family. From the standpoint of national welfare there is no virtue to be ascribed to one or another method. The point of economic waste may quite logically be advanced to show that expensive funerals are not "American" in any true sense.

What we have, then, is a set of assumptions that are quite legitimate if they fit into the system of values of a family. Observance of them as against opposing assumptions and value systems is in no sense socially obligatory, or necessarily desirable. Let us see how these six assumptions are advocated by the funeral industry. We have seen the organizational structure through which the leaders work. Next to be observed is the spirit in which the fundamental convictions are upheld, and the attitudes presented to the public.

An attitude involving much more than the usual degree of defensiveness is to be found in the very great majority of funeral directors, and in the articles and editorials of the journals. It is aggravated by the books such as that of Gebhart, *Funeral Costs* (see Chapter V) and articles on the subject that appear occasionally in popular magazines. More than this one cause, it would seem, is needed to explain the universality of the defensiveness. More than likely the following factors influence the attitude: the place of the funeral director in the community, the peripheral relationship of the business to institutions, and the continuous resistance of a part of the public to the claims for a professional status for the vocation. Once in a while an article will appear in a trade journal, or a speech will be made at a funeral directors' meeting, saying, in effect: why do we react so violently to a book such as Evelyn Waugh's *The Loved One*? Or, we don't deserve criticism; we have no secrets to hide.

The evidences of the defensive attitude do not lessen. At the November, 1955, convention of the National Funeral Directors Association, it is reported that the members were warned not to become unduly alarmed by criticisms appearing in the "confidential" type of magazine; they are best ignored. Further, the members were told that some of these magazines are under investigation by the Post Office or are being sued for slander. One of the outstanding services the associations and the journals render the whole industry, as related by many undertakers, is that of being a watch dog to prevent, silence, or as a last recourse, to answer, any unfavorable comment about themselves. A striking article that appeared in the *American Funeral Director* in 1948 told of a public relations team made up of representatives of the New York metropolitan association, the funeral supply trade, and the editors of two prominent funeral trade journals, cooperating by telephone and letter with representatives of the National Funeral Directors Association. The association officers and others on the team learn about stories that may appear in magazines and contact the writers in an attempt to see the stories and check for errors. An interesting case is cited in which the editorial staff of a magazine, after being interviewed by one of the team, abandoned the proposed publication project. (9, p. 48)

To funeral directors public relations seems to be a one-way street. They feel rather strongly that information about funerals should come only from them, despite the fact that other persons are affected. There are other legitimate, honest, and not necessarily antagonistic viewpoints, but the funeral directors almost invariably answer any statement about opinions at variance with their own, with a repetition of their familiar defenses. It is this intransigeance which threatens most the hope that in the present organized system of undertakers a more satisfactory procedure at funerals can be found.

Since criticism from outside is rejected or resented, and since there must be some basis for the complaints levelled at funeral directors, the question arises: do the practitioners discipline their own miscreant colleagues, and how do they do it? It is almost impossible to get reliable and adequate information on the first part of the question. It would allay suspicion on the part of the critics if a frank statement were made publicly at stated periods of action taken to reduce the evils reported. Instead the point is made over and over by spokesmen for the industry that the charges are true of only a small minority of unethical operators. The majority of operators are sincere, honest, and strictly ethical, they say. The critic is usually accused of maligning the whole industry by citing cases of wrong doing. Since discipline is largely in the hands of the industry, and since also its leaders usually know which ones among the practitioners are guilty, the surest way to give to the public a sense of trust in the majority, would lie in factual assurance that it is disciplining its own ranks.

The types of wrong doing occur with convincing repetition as the writers among the undertakers themselves complain. They are of the kind that could be dealt with: excessive charges, particularly of families whose welfare for months or years in the future is harmed, collusion in fixing and raising prices, padding of services, suppression of information on costs, extensive ex parte lobbying, and many others. Funeral directors are frequently urged by their own leaders to ignore the accusations since only a minority of customers is victimized. The managing director of National Selected Morticians made the statement that the number dismissed from membership in that group amounted to something like one a year. It would be reassuring if the public could be informed as to the number in all associations who are induced to desist from exploitative practices.

Two methods of influencing member practices are open to the associations on municipal or state level. The first is to have pressure brought on the guilty firm to live up to the terms of the code of ethics. The code in most instances enjoins fair play with clients, competitors, and employees; honest representation of merchandise costs; guarding of confidences by clients; and helpful conduct to advance associational effort, legislative provisions and public relations. Seldom are the provisions in the code spelled out in concrete terms as is done in the case of the Ohio Funeral Directors Association. There are instances in which officers of associations have appealed privately, with or without reference to the code, to practitioners known to be grossly unfair. How often this happens is difficult to ascertain.

The most effective method utilized by state and local associations to induce the worst offenders to change their ways, or to leave the vocation, is to appeal to the state authority to consider revocation of the license of the guilty party. Few licensees are deprived of their right to practice.

Since the undertakers are not an intimate part of the social structure of the community, it is to be expected that they will use outside channels to obtain their ends in communities. State legislation is the most useful way, and hence it is utilized to the full. It is ideal in one regard especially: through lobbying it can be used to get results without much public notice. The funeral industry is very successful in its lobbying efforts. The curious law in California requiring that all ashes of cremated remains be kept permanently in urns at registered cemeteries or mausoleums, was backed in passage by the funeral industry. Its terms forbid the scattering of human ashes over water or cherished spots of earth. At the 1955 convention of the National Funeral Directors Association it was reported that in three years of sponsorship by the association, more than one-half the states had adopted legislation controlling the sale of "pre-need" funerals. As has been noted, legislation in some states require that bodies be cremated in caskets.

In one other way the associations have utilized state government machinery to the advantage of the industry. From their earliest days the national and state associations have exercised a continuous and successful influence on state legislatures to set standards of "licensure" for embalmers and funeral directors. The mortuary schools have grown in number and importance partly because of the licensing requirements. The Conference of Funeral Examining Boards, Incorporated has served as an instrument through which the industry has worked to standardize and elevate the level of training in the nineteen conference accredited schools.

Committees on education and coordinating associations of the schools have added their weight to the efforts of the groups described above to bring some unity into the state licensing laws, to improve curricular offerings, to bring about broader educational training before entrance to the schools, and to improve apprenticeship experience.

A further characteristic of the thinking of the undertaking group must be spoken of in order to complete an outline of its assumptions, its discipline and its ideology. Intimately bound up with the attitudes of funeral directors toward the conduct of the funeral and toward the statement of their case to the public, are their concepts of control over funeral activity throughout the nation, and the place of the industry in the national power structure. In essence they believe that the conduct of all funerals should be in the hands of, and controlled by private competitive proprietors like themselves. Public ownership or participation is anathema to them, including even the contract service of two mortuaries in Veteran Administration hospitals. Government regulation comes in for no more favorable consideration. The associations are hailed as part of a great experiment in democracy; a bulwark against government regulations. No discrepancy is seen between opposition to federal regulation and their own advocacy of state governmental control over licensing. This form of state control may be different from government regulation in their eyes because undertakers themselves constitute a large portion of the personnel of the state boards.

Private cooperative enterprise is disliked by funeral directors, although their printed statements on the subject take on a milder tone than their oral utterances. The burden of the arguments against consumer cooperatives rests first on the mistaken assumption that all such enterprises are free of many tax burdens, second that a funeral of as good quality as offered by the cooperatives will be furnished by any competitive establishment at the same price, and third that the competitive business provides funerals free of charge for indigent families.

The charitable cases take a large place in the ideology of the undertaker as an argument for private competitive as over against public or cooperative enterprise. Undoubtedly the charity involved is given with greater willingness because it is a protection against entrance into the field of funerals by official agencies and is an argument against cooperative funeral enterprise.

Undertaker leaders and writers identify their business with the private enterprise system. The speakers at association conventions and the writers for journals are not content with statements of loyalty to free enterprise. They often appear to need an object of hostility, even of vituperation. Communists and communism serve the purpose quite suitably.

The next step some of them take is to relate all opposition to themselves and their ideas to Communism. Not all within the industry indulge in the game, but all too frequently statements like this are made:

" . . . this publication definitely is convinced that there is a more or less organized 'inner circle' of influence . . . (it) has as one of its objects destruction of the American Way of Life, including the American Way of Burial.

"It is from this group, or its sympathizers, that most of the criticism of funeral service, the cost of it and the like, originates." (10, p. 8)

Communists may criticize funerals in the United States; presumably they do. However, the great majority of the undertaker's critics are not communistic.

Summary. The key to many of the assumptions made by funeral directors and the methods used by them is the over-abundance of establishments in the country. This fact and the relatively stable annual number of deaths creates the need for higher return for each funeral if the majority of firms are to survive. The common predicament of the great majority of funeral establishments creates a great need for organization on a national scale to bring about unity in the industry and a rationale for funerals at prices high enough to bring the desired amount of profit. The lack of strong functional relations of funeral establishments along with the marginal place of the undertaker in the community lead him to compensate by following rigidly the norms of the business and conducting himself in accordance with the value system adopted by the business as a whole.

Great uniformity exists among undertakers in the assumptions they hold of the values of display at funerals and the methods they use to induce bereaved families to accept them. Uniformity is extensive despite wide geographical spread, intense competition, class and cultural differences. This unity is engendered largely by the leaders working through national associations. The five associations all promulgate the same core assumptions having to do with elaborate funerals. However each association advocates its own methods of elevating standards and eventually reducing the numbers of operators in the business. Two of the associations serve the special needs of the Jewish and Negro cultural groups.

The organizational structure is both strong and adaptable. Through state and local associations the national groups exert great influence throughout the industry. Internal discipline is exercised through pressure by local groups to live up to the ideals of the codes of ethics. The public which hears, through other sources, of exploitation of families by unscrupulous practitioners, rarely hears of disciplinary action against them. The assocations, under the guidance of apt leadership, have accomplished a great deal for the trade, through advocacy and counseling in the establishment of state licensing laws, and through lobbying for laws to protect and further the interests of the individual operators. The leaders and the trade journals assume a very defensive attitude toward any expression of criticism. They identify themselves with private profit enterprise and oppose private cooperative funeral enterprise and any public funeral service or regulation other than through licensing.

The funeral business is ably led and very effectively organized. It operates largely outside community influences and has achieved legislative results with a minimum of attention from the public.

CHANGES IN FORM AND FUNCTIONS

CHAPTER IX

"INFLUENCES OF CULTURAL CHANGE"

The ever-whirling wheele of change, the which all mortall things doth sway.
                                        EDMUND SPENSER

In Part III a different perspective on funerals is taken in order to get at a third dimension of the subject. In Part I the first observations were made to get bearings; to look at the phenomenon as it occurred, and to note the sequence of happenings of a funeral; that is, to get a word picture of the action pattern. In Part II the object was to slip behind the pattern of happenings on the screen; to discover the pressures on parties in the funeral situation arising in the family and other institutional and community settings; to look for motivations arising out of the pressures; and thus to develop a concept of the inter-acting forces working in persons and groups to form the complex of forces that produce the funeral as we saw it in action in Part I. In essence Part II was an attempt to draw a cross section of the mechanism of the funeral at a given period; and at the same time to see what forces of individual desire and social constraint operate through the mechanism; and lastly, so far as possible, to gauge the strength of the forces as they operate.

Part III will attempt to discover how the whole machinery changes, or is changed, as time elapses, and in what ways individual motivations and social pressures may seem to act differently now than in an earlier era. If Part II can be called a flat, cross sectional view, Part III is the recording of developments beneath it, and a projection of expectations of developments above it. To the perspective of a set of relationships, depth and a better understanding of the significance of the funeral to individuals and society may be gained by a time perspective.

A portrayal of the funeral from the angle of the developments that occur in it in the course of decades reveals a second major distinction between Part III and the sections preceding it. While Part I dealt with the actions and other happenings to all participants in the course of the series of gatherings in the narrow funeral complex, and Part II dealt with specific, sectional relations within the total funeral situation, in Part III the assumption is that a comprehension of each of these will be carried in mind and fitted into a sweeping view of the national society in transition from one period to another. Part II covers inter group relations; Part III social, or, more correctly, cultural patterns of relationships. It will not be a long sweep; the period covered is historically brief, since the nation-wide developments which have most importantly modified funeral practices have been recent and rapid.

Part III represents an effort to assess the status of the funeral in present day society; to discover in what aspects it has lost or gained meaning for the participants, and in what ways, if any, it might be supplemented to become a more significant experience. It is necessary in the interests of clear understanding to reemphasize the approach taken in this study to the problem in hand. It is a social point of view assuming, but not analyzing, the features of the ceremony regarded as sacred. The only exceptions are the funeral experiences in which the absence of clerical conduct of the ritual has been noted. Not only have I a deep respect for the loyalties and commitments of persons of faiths other than my own; not only have I frequently and continuously found inspiration by participating in some of the church activities of these persons, and hence regard the strictly religious or sacred observance as of the utmost and compelling importance—not only that, but in the strictly objective fact-finding stage of the study, I have discovered that a faith sincerely held gave the greatest solace, and provided the deepest meaning at this period.

In Part III the needs of bereaved persons caused by the loss of an intimate friend or associate are described. They are to be found in the minds of members of churches and synagogues, and also in the minds of those professing allegiance to no religious organizations or beliefs. I have treated them as human needs and have shown the desirability of meeting them by whatever methods and through whatever channels are most appropriate in individual instances. Where they fall, as they often do, within the realm of the sacred for any family, it goes without saying, that the ecclesiastical institution is the channel for their expression. It does not detract from the priority of the church in this respect, if there are secular contexts in which some of these needs ought also to be met to give to bereaved persons a rounded sense of satisfaction.

Since the funeral of today is to be compared in Part III with that of the past, it becomes necessary to state the criteria on which comparison is to be based. This is particularly the case because of the fundamental difference between the bases of progress assumed in this study and those assumed by the leaders among funeral directors. One of the chief claims made by them is that the modern funeral in all of its temporal aspects shows very great improvement over its antecedent form. The basis of the claim lies largely in the realm of the elegance of materials and the modernity of equipment used. On that score the facts compel agreement; the modern funeral is much more costly and pretentious. The comparison I will attempt to make in Part III will be along entirely different lines, namely, the degree to which the funeral serves the deeper needs of the bereaved individual and the community in which it takes place. It is upon the matter of the function that it performs that the present study has laid emphasis. It has to do with emotions and their satisfactions, and with the effect of the series of funeral happenings on family, group and community. The element of display and mechanical efficiency may or may not have a part in the effect that is made, but the basic criterion of excellence will be functional efficiency within the social grouping.

Chapter X

EFFECTS OF CITY CIVILIZATION

The past is like a funeral gone by,
The Future comes like an unwelcome guest.
EDMUND GOSSE

The present factory and city civilization in the United States differs from the farm and small community civilization of a few generations ago. As scientific and technological discoveries resulted in machines, and machines in factories, the factories drew men and their families to jobs in growing cities and to a kind of life that was new to them. Old habits had to be changed when prescribed work at a machine during stipulated hours took the place of hard but family-determined tasks and hours on the farm. The pace of life quickened, the spaciousness of the old gave way to the crowdedness of the new. The time-honored traditions which every one knew, did not work so well in the city, some of them not at all. Most particularly, the ways of relaxing together that characterized rural life were not appropriate in the city. In many other ways city life demanded change in the thought and action of the new comers.

Among the large scale developments within the population of cities that changed the social atmosphere was the influx of greater numbers of immigrants brought by opportunities for jobs in factories. The peoples who came were from countries whose ways of life differed in large measure from that of the North European countries of earlier immigration. Ethnic and religious differences were sharper and more numerous; and, in the proximity of diverse customs and faiths, a further cause arose to bring into question the old convictions, habits and assurances. Life in cities was not merely a shift from habits, usages and routines; it involved a strain on the sense of adequacy of city dwellers to face the more intangible problems. Most devastating was the break in the ways in which individuals associated with each other, in family relations, in social gatherings, in the mutual interests or separation of youth from their elders. The strain of adjustment made itself felt, then, both in superficial and material ways, also on social and psychic levels.

It was not alone the cities which felt the impact of industrialism or even of urbanism. The city, invaded from the small towns and the open country, developed the seeds of a new culture, and with them, in turn invaded the rural areas from which its inhabitants had come. Science flourished in the concentrations of people, and so also did the centers of art and culture. For these the non-city folk were as eager as their urban cousins. Science and technology along with other advances made transportation and communication rapid, easy, and extensively available. Railroads, highways, automobiles, airplanes, telegraph, telephone, radio, television, motion pictures, brought the words, actions, problems and strains of the city to the rural areas. Today the latter are "citified," only in less degree than the cities. Urbanism is at present not a matter of city as over against the country side, but a matter rather of degree, with its most intense concentration in metropolises, its least in the out of the way places.

All this is not only pertinent to the study of modern funerals; it is basic. The remainder of this chapter explains the effects of the industrial and social changes of the last century on the form and meaning of the funeral.

Misfit of Old Funeral Forms to Urban Conditions. As towns in America grew in size and number the part played in funerals by the undertaker increased in scope and responsibility. In the earliest colonial days, and until considerably later in isolated rural or cultural communities, members of the family and neighbors performed all the tasks consequent to death. The washing of the body and its "laying out" were the first tasks usually done by a member of the intimate family group but not infrequently by a friendly neighbor. The male members of the family dug the grave, if it was to be located in a family plot on the farm, or the sexton did, if the body was to be interred in the churchyard. The coffin containing the body was carried by family members, neighbors and friends to the church; and those closest to the deceased, or the sexton, filled the grave after the coffin had been lowered. The funeral was a family and neighborhood affair, taking place in the home.

Increasingly thereafter family conditions developed that made the home funeral less suitable and the role of the family somewhat different from that of the 1860's and '70's. Housing quarters for the family were, by and large, much more limited in space; stairways and foyers created problems for the moving of caskets; parlors or living rooms were too small to accommodate the visitors at the wake and funeral assemblages. In such restricted quarters to keep the body in the living rooms for two or three days created serious problems. Families became smaller decade by decade, and near dwellers less neighborly. Consequently there were fewer whose daily personal relations were disturbed by the death, fewer to take part in the duties of the funeral according to the former custom. Relatives, even those of close connection with the immediate family, were scattered, and either could not come long distances, or found living accommodations difficult or expensive. In another sense the home became less suitable for the funeral gatherings: the family's circle of acquaintances was increasingly made up of persons met in a number of various relationships, relatively few of whom were familiar with the home. The funeral assemblage became a wider, more ephemeral group of acquaintances. To meet these several difficulties the funeral home became more and more the place of preparation of the body, for holding the wake, and in a fraction of cases, for the final ritual.

The metamorphosis in the community brought about by the growth of cities has affected the funeral as much as or more than has the change in the family. In the earliest days the funeral was as much a community as a family matter, when the community consisted of a closely knit, geographically isolated group of families. Occupations were less diverse than later, and unusual events were treated as community responsibilities. Death of an individual was a deprivation of customary social give and take to a large proportion of the total group, and a matter of common knowledge and discussion of all. The loss of one life was a distinctly felt diminution of the total community. In cities, the family found itself in a much more limited relationship to nearby families; neighborhood activities and neighborly relations became less and less real.

In a small community, particularly one which is centered around agricultural vocations and interests, attendance at funerals can be decided by individuals. In cities, factory and office workers are subject to comparatively inflexible rules regulating working hours, and attendance at a funeral of any one but a relative is forbidden or is granted only at the expense of a day's pay. One result has been greater emphasis on the wake to which workers may go in the evening. The country over, it is estimated that there is a larger attendance at wakes than at funeral services. The funeral home, having more of a public and less of an intimate flavor, fits into the pattern of community relationships better than does the family home.

Of more importance, however, for the conduct of the funeral, is the loss of person to person communication of information about the death and the funeral. It becomes known in much larger measure through the obituary notices in the daily papers. However, because of the cost, not every funeral is advertised in the papers and many are noted in only one or a few such daily periodicals. The news articles of deaths cover a very few of all the deaths, since the large number are of little news value. As a consequence, as city culture becomes more prevalent, a smaller proportion of friends and acquaintances learn of the occurrence of death before the funeral takes place. This is true in general even when individual notices are sent out by the family, since the trend is toward smaller lists of notices. From these, as well as other causes, the community aspect that looms so large in funerals of the past, especially those in small centers, has very greatly diminished.

The Jewish funeral, like all others, originally was communal. Every one was expected to come. The transition to the more urban allocation of responsibilities and pattern of attendance has resulted in a special group, the Hevrah Kadisha, representing the community. It assumes some of the roles enacted in former days by relatives and neighbors; in some communities it performs certain phases of preparation of the body; in other communities it functions only in the charitable provision of appropriate funerals for needy persons within the group.

The settlement of minority groups in cities has brought about an uncertainty in the minds of many citizens concerning the proprieties to be followed. Each cultural group has had its own peculiarities of mortuary practices, adapting in time to a more "American" pattern. In the process not only the members of these groups but all citizens have become less certain of the proper procedures to follow. Older Americans in the closely knit smaller communities were familiar with the roles that relatives, friends and neighbors formerly played; but as the knowledge proved inadequate in cities, uncertainty succeeded assurance. In consequence the funeral director, more than willing to instruct, became a feature more essential than before.

Urbanization has taken its toll from the churches also, through the influence of high mobility which has characterized an industrialized, urban civilization. In a rural economy families remain for years, and even generations, rooted in one locality, often retaining an old homestead for many decades. In cities factory jobs, commercial and professional positions, coupled with the compulsion of shifting neighborhoods, compel frequent changes of residence. As families move, church affiliations are broken, and connections in new locations delayed or neglected. Thus it happens that the church, which with the family and the community formed the combination of institutions that made the funeral an important event, has lost much of its influence over the ritual for a large number of people. The multiplicity of organizations in urban areas has indirectly worked toward that end in smaller measure. A fraternal or patriotic order, while not in any sense opposed to church-conducted funerals, may take charge of the service. In some cases in which conflict on the selection of minister arises between members of the family affiliated with different faiths, compromise is made by agreeing upon a ceremony under a fraternal order to which the deceased belonged.

Adaptations Made by the Funeral Industry. The folkways which governed the roles of the attendants and the procedures to be followed in rural areas and small towns in the United States were inapplicable in the industrialized culture of the cities. In the new conditions in the cities, in the heterogeneous mass of people and the number and variety of national origins, there was no common cultural background on which to base a new set of practices applicable to all. There was something of a vacuum, into which the burial entrepreneur moved and began to formulate custom to his own liking.

The funeral business is the last to appear in a growing community among the economic services. In a study of 101 cities: "Coefficients of correlation were calculated between population and the number of each kind of economic service in the community . . . on the basis of frequency of persons per single economic service one might predict the probable order of appearance of each kind of economic service in a small, growing community. According to the present study, the economic services that would be among the first to appear are the food stores, doctor and filling station. The economic service of dry goods store and funeral director would be the last to appear." (1, pp. 60-62) Because, in part, undertaking as a business came late to developing and changing communities, it was unhindered by tradition from rapid adaptation to urban conditions.

Funeral directing, itself a product of urban development, has adapted its practices to make the most of the opportunity to mold a mass culture for funerals. As a full-time vocation of any considerable number of practitioners it is something less than one hundred years old, having grown out of vocations in which occasional services directly related to funerals were given. Among them were the trade of the carpenter who made the early coffins for the family, the cabinet maker, the livery man, the sexton. For many years undertaking was combined with one or more other types of business to furnish a living and an outlet for all the skills of the proprietor. During the Civil War the greatest impetus to undertaking was provided in the need to preserve the remains of those killed in combat until they could be delivered to their families and buried. Concoction of embalming fluids and experiments in embalming had been pursued for years prior to that time and by several individuals. The war gave the opportunity for further experimentation, a measure of perfection in the process, and a foothold for a full-time vocation. From the time of its close the leadership in the development of embalming passed from chemists and physicians to embalming companies and undertakers. (2) This has become increasingly evident.

Embalming laid the basis for the continued and increasing emphasis on the body at the funeral. Through its effects, the body could be retained above ground longer and more safely than through the use of ice to preserve it. Embalming afforded also the opportunity for, and basic method of, "restoring" the facial features of the dead to a likeness to the living face. "Beautification" and elaboration of accessories to the laid-out body developed rapidly from that historic point on. Embalming, itself an inexpensive operation, opened the way for the development and expansion of the methods that in part have resulted in increasingly costly funerals.

A second technical development that helped materially to pave the way for an expanded industry was the adoption, at about the end of the first decade of the century, of motorized hearses and cars. Motor hearses were expensive, especially as changes in style necessitated repeated replacements. Nevertheless, use of them lessened the burden of the procession to the cemetery which had to cover long distances as the city cemeteries were moved from central areas to outskirts, and even beyond city limits.

Pride of bereaved families in following out the folkways surrounding the funeral, and the satisfaction of friends and neighbors in their roles on such occasion had increasingly to be relinquished in city environments. As a substitute funeral attendants were offered passive participation in an event, or series of events, the arrangements of which were largely in the hands of a specialist. Passive observation nearly always leads to expectations of more spectacular performance than does active participation. The commercial drive of the funeral director for more elegance and display therefore fitted the need for a substitute for the folk habits involving active participation of previous years. In one other way transition to city life made the modern funeral acceptable to families. In cities they became accustomed to paying for services they previously had performed themselves. And with the rise in their standard of living they had money to pay for the services.

The funeral establishment, too, has followed a pattern of adaptation to city conditions. At first, especially in the east, stores were used. Later large residences were taken over as they became available in changing residential areas and finally, new buildings were erected as funeral establishments. Variations in the stages at which the sequence begins, occur in different parts of the country, but the progression has been consistently toward the elegent, costly and stylish building.

Equipment for funerals has steadily increased in mechanical excellence and coverage of detailed needs. Materials, mechanisms and specific services have multiplied along with the decline in the control over the conduct of funerals by family, church and community. The funeral director has succeeded in filling with material and pecuniary values the gap made by the social values expressed in neighborly concern and active complementary roles.

Cremation as a means of disposing of the remains is one adaptation to urban conditions that is utilized in a minority of instances. The cremation movement has not been fostered by the funeral directors' association nor the trade journals, but has been independently led. It arose out of the concern for the problem of increasing space needed for burial plots as cities grew in size. In the early stages of the movement its proponents were disturbed also by the problem of sanitation, presenting itself as an accumulation of dead human bodies a few feet underground in the enlarging cemeteries. Following its first consideration in England discussion of the question in the United States became most active during the last three quarters of the nineteenth century and the early years of the twentieth.

The two aspects of the problem have never been met completely. The question of space has been solved temporarily, and in part only, by the conversion of tracts at the periphery or outside city limits to cemetery use. The problem of sanitation involved in numerous burials has been met partially by the same action, but more particularly by modern sanitary provisions.

However, the chief significance of cremation is of a different nature. It is the one technical development that serves to redress the imbalance of bargaining power between undertaker and customer, by counteracting the emphasis on the body and allowing for a more wholesome attitude toward the funeral on the part of the family. Logically resort to cremation eliminates the need of embalming, "restoration," and lavish expenditures for casket and all funeral "goods," but allows for all the social and spiritual aspects of the funeral period. The only objection to its use, and it is a formidable one, is its failure to satisfy the religious requirements of Catholics and Orthodox Jews. One obstacle to its use, gradually being overcome, is the inaccessibility of crematories in certain cities in the country.

Because of the ease, dispatch and thoroughness of the process, it is favored by a large majority of the intellectual group in the population, with the exception of those whose religious commitments prohibit its use. The undertaking industry opposes or discourages its use for obvious reasons, going to the unfair and ridiculous limit, as we have seen, of successful advocacy of state laws to require that cremation take place only when the body is enclosed in a casket. Nevertheless the utilization of cremation is steadily increasing throughout the country. (See Appendix III)

Functions of the Funeral in Small and Large Communities. The subject of the adequacy of the conduct of funerals and the values involved in it which help meet the needs of present-day society leads directly to considerations of function. What results does it achieve for individuals, the family, groups, the community? What effects are actually experienced by the participants? The most universal feature of all funerals, excepting only the disposal of the body and the religious ceremony, is the assembling of relatives, friends and neighbors of the deceased, or in strongly coherent groups, the assembling of all the members. It has been said by social scientists that in societies less developed than our own, there is a desire, stimulated by the death, to reexperience total group association. The same desire in modified forms is to be found in modern society. To bring the whole group together is the accepted tradition in this country when death comes to a member.

The function performed by the gatherings in small communities—i.e., the strengthening of the sense of community solidarity—is real, if not great. Persons of various faiths, of various vocations and economic levels come together in the wake or at the religious service. They have an experience that, from all the evidence, is fraught more with a recognition of participation in a total network of community relations, than is felt by attendants in cities.

The larger the town the more the gatherings at wakes and rituals lose significance for the community as a whole to become occasions on which groups may derive a modicum of added coherence. In this respect much depends on the strength of the already existing bond between the members, and on the relative isolation from the larger community. Among certain minority groups, for example, a funeral brings together representatives of all the organizations and societies, and a very large number of all the adults of the ethnic community. As in the case of the village or small town, there is seldom any tangible result other than a slightly intensified sense of coherence of the nationality group. This result is to be observed even among a people who may be scattered in several pockets of population throughout a metropolis.

It is impossible, in the face of all the evidence, to ascribe to the funeral any but a small effect in knitting communities or groups together, an effect seen at its maximum in small communities and isolated groups. For the most part, even in these social segments, it serves merely to reassert momentarily an existing solidarity. The effect upon the family is not as fugitive. The funeral serves in many cases in which the immediate family or near relatives are scattered to bring them together and to renew and strengthen the family tie.

The result most frequently mentioned as intended or desired by the family from the series of events before burial, is status or prestige for itself, achieved supposedly through display of costly casket, flowers and other features of the funeral. To evaluate this function, or to measure it by comparison of instances occurring under diverse circumstances is difficult. Many persons take great pride in the elegance of funerals for which they have been responsible. If the pride or other satisfaction is great and enduring enough to balance the loss of returns from money that might have been used for other purposes, then clearly costly types of funerals are justified from their standpoint. It is a matter of the values that are to be associated with a "fine" as opposed to a modest showing.

There is at least this much of the undertaker's point of view on the matter of costs that cannot be gainsaid: it is not extravagance on the part of the client to follow the course that in the end gives greatest returns to him. Nor is it exploitation on the part of the seller to persuade him to choose the style of funeral if he, the seller, is certain it will provide the greatest satisfaction. There is, however, a great preponderance of evidence that he cannot be sure that the funeral he provides does answer the need of the family in any deep sense. The brief period of the burial procedures, the unusual state of mind and consequent temporarily twisted set of values of the client family during that period, and the pressures bearing on them during the moments of choice, render their judgments at the time less reliable than at other times.

Many complain bitterly later that they would have decided on more modest funerals if they had been given unfettered choice. Many who have had to lower their standard of living because of a lavish funeral have discovered that their decisions have not been based on rational assessment of the lasting value of funerals to the family. There is very serious question that the lasting returns from the expensive funeral are commensurate with the outlay in any but a limited number of instances.

The wished for result of large expenditures is the elevation of the status of the family in the community of acquaintances. But rarely is the status of a family raised in the opinion of neighbors and friends by ostentation at a funeral. Almost invariably it is recognized as conspicuous display, whether it is approved or not. Occasionally acquaintances predict a lowering in the standard of living of a family and with it a somewhat lower status. Or, even though the participants enjoy an elaborate wake and funeral, in their eyes the standing of the family may be lowered, if to furnish it the family has had to accept charity from some source.

There are circumstances, however, in which lavish, costly funerals bring to the family much attention from fellow members of the group or "set" of which they are a part. For a brief span of time the surviving family members become the center of social activity, as happens in some immigrant groups at certain stages of assimilation. Nevertheless, even in these cases judgment concerning the family's permanent status must be exercised with caution. In the first place the funeral may be looked upon as just another show and "party," the like of which any one of a large number of families is expected to put on under similar circumstances. In the second place, among certain minority groups, a substantial portion of the cost of the affair is contributed by those who take part, and they therefore have less feeling of being outclassed than might otherwise be the case.

Unusual circumstances may result in isolated instances in which the neighbors have come to a realization for the first time of the worth of a family through the medium of a funeral, especially in the case of a very retiring household. Except in small communities, however, the funeral held by an obscure family usually goes unnoticed. The smaller the community the more will be known about the status to be ascribed to any family funeral.

Under certain circumstances a funeral may bring a great deal of prestige to a family, sometimes with a measure of permanence. Such is the case when the funeral of a member of an organization is used for the aggrandizement of the whole group. For example, the funeral of a relative of an official in a religious denomination may be the occasion to have outstanding leaders attend; and in other ways to make the wake and ceremony notable. More often, a political organization may demonstrate its strength by directing the attendance of hundreds of government officials who owe their positions to it. In cases of this kind it cannot be said that the funeral achieves status for the deceased, or for the family, but rather that the organization confers status on the funeral. It is also true that the status acquired is not due to costly and elaborate materials but to group action. If, then, achievement of status is a function of the funeral, it is at best a thin and brittle blessing.

The third and only other important social or functional value of the funeral is that of strengthening the basic rules of life in the convictions and habits of the persons assembled at the wake and ceremony. There is no questioning the fact that at a funeral largely attended by loyal members of a church or other group, or by the residents of long standing in a small town, there is a focusing of emphasis on the old, established ideals. The group turns back to the older norms of group living. The group, as a whole, does not turn to the more problematical areas of need for formulation of ideals for a changing situation. It is reaffirmation of faith, sacred and secular, that they experience.

In a situation, however, in which the majority in the group, or the dominant leaders, are engaged in a struggle to elevate the status of the group or to correct a social injustice that oppresses them, or in other ways to conduct a campaign for change in government, labor relations, religion, education or any other field, the group turns at a funeral to a reaffirmation of the new faith. In such situations, aside from its identifying purpose, the members of the group are often more heterogeneous than in funerals of the kind described.   In both cases, far more than in other funerals, the size of the group enhances the intensity of group reaction.

The third function of the funeral, then, the strengthening of devotion to group ideals, operates in those cases in which the ideals are accepted.   In a very large number of funerals of individuals neither devoutly orthodox or socially progressive, little group sense of ideals is to be met.   In such cases probing reveals a variety of individual reactions.   Not infrequently, however, doubts and arguments come forth. In the car, on the way to or from the cemetary, or later in informal groups, conflicting opinions on an individual basis are expressed about the advantage of living a righteous life.   In such cases it would seem that the death had raised the question of ideals, but the group had come up with no convincing answers.   At times like these, however, the discussants often express a sense of "release" following their remarks about moral and ethical convictions.

Two other items are mentioned from time to time as functions of the funeral.   One is purging of an emotional kind through wailing or other public expression of grief.   It is a practice surviving in very few cultural groups.   It is certain that some individuals especially members of the immediate family, find satisfaction in wailing when it is the expected thing to do.   That it lessens grief at all is not so certain.   In the groups in which it has been the custom many of the younger generation, who look on it as mere role playing, are irritated by it.   It is not universal enough to regard it seriously as a main function of the funeral.   Nor is there sufficient evidence to say that any positive results come from it.   At best, it befits a closely knit cultural group into which has not yet permeated the tradition of restraining emotion in public.

In certain Pentecostal groups in cities and in some out of the way communities, outbursts of revelry are stimulated by a funeral in which the whole group finds occasion to indulge in riotous activity, sometimes for days. (3, pp. 650-654)   In the urban groups, at least, the experience is very similar to those stimulated by happenings other than death, except that emotional expressions reach a higher peak than they do at Sunday or mid-week outbursts.   They may also last for a longer period.

A fifth function observed occasionally, especially by ministers, is the public pronouncement of the end of a life and the stamping of all former relations with the deceased with the "seal of finality." It is true that witnessing the lowering of the casket and the filling of the grave over it leaves a clear impression of finality. However its importance is lessened by the fact that an ever diminishing number witness the rite. That the committal service is of consequence, even to family or friends is questionable, except where it is essential in the religious ritual. A much more useful instrumentality to impress the finality of death on the community is the obituary notice in the newspaper. In the small, well knit group or community no ceremonial marking of the end is needed. Lastly it is questionable if a ritualistic assertion that relations with the deceased are at an end is important under modern urban conditions. City dwellers have learned the art of making and breaking, or at least taking lightly in their stride, the multiplicity of ephemeral relationships.

As size of the community is one variable that determines in part the effectiveness of the funeral, another is the relative prominence of the deceased within the group or in the community. The death of a leader affects the members partly because it influences the achievements of the group as a whole, but mostly because it disrupts the continuing responses to him. In consequence the funeral becomes a total group affair in the measure in which the dead leader was felt to be important in group affairs and in the degree he was known by the members.

Prominence of the deceased in the community or the larger society greatly affects the attendance at the funeral. At the lower end of the scale of prominence is the young child whose funeral is planned very simply, costs relatively little and is attended by few. Its effect in the community is small. At the upper end of the scale is the person whose name is known to all, and whose acts have been watched by thousands. He may be a statesman, artist, prize fighter, baseball player or gangster. According to the measure of his fame or notoriety his funeral will be attended by masses of persons, and descriptions of it will be read widely.

The nature of his life activities determines the type of individuals who make up the bulk of the attendants at his funeral. However, curiosity and the excitement of the crowd usually dominate the demonstration attending the funerals of the notorious, the appeal of whose lives has been to the most primitive ideas and practices. Sometimes the mass attendance is used by an organized group for its own aggrandizement, as is sometimes exemplified in the conduct of one or another branch of gangsterism when one of its leaders is buried. The funeral of a statesman, on the other hand, serves to magnify the ideals and basic purposes of the total society.

Whenever the funeral celebrates the life and work of a person in a group too large to encompass the reliving of face to face collective experiences, it assumes a character different from the usual funeral. That it has a function cannot be gainsaid; but that function is so different in emphasis as to alter its fundamental nature. It becomes a public ceremonial, leaving to the family and close friends the need of the more intimate get together that the usual funeral answers. It may be a mass demonstration approximating the characteristics of a mob, and possessing little but very momentary effect. Paradoxically, the effect of the mass demonstration is almost invariably restricted, giving a certain release of a strictly emotional nature. The ideal funeral influences individuals in a contrary fashion.

One type of misfortune demonstrates the failure of large-city culture to provide a ritual to alleviate the suddenly aroused apprehension of large numbers of persons. The misfortune may come to an individual or to a group, and always involves the revelation of a danger that may befall any one who habitually follows the course of action in which the victim, or victims, met their crisis. Examples include the tragedy of a kidnaped child, the drowning of a child in waters under public jurisdiction, the death of a number of children in a cave-in of earth thrown up in the process of construction, an unsolved murder of a citizen engaged in a laudable pursuit. Through the press, radio and television the fears of masses of people are aroused, and often kept alive for days. Invariably the question of responsibility becomes acute, and investigations are started by private and public agencies.

The funeral in such a case usually becomes a focus of public attention, and may attract an unusually large attendance. Nevertheless, the many thousands, or even millions, who have been disturbed by the death and whose assurance in certain of the collective processes is shaken, are afforded only the slight satisfaction of expressing themselves in a small circle of friends and listening to their fears in reply. True, the tragedy may increase public pressure eventually to correct wholly or in part the defect in provisions for the common safety. And yet the need of interaction between affected individuals which the funeral provides in small groups, is not, and cannot be furnished on a large scale.

The possibility of devising a mass ritual is always present, but its processes and effects are not of the kind to perform the function of a constructive ritual, valuable though they may be in other ways. The main defect in them, from the standpoint of human interaction, lies in the fact that action in masses takes only one direction. People are talked to, and not heard, in meetings, in the press and over the radio. Interpersonal or intergroup discourse is difficult if not impossible, as is member-leader interaction.

The funeral of a prominent person may involve little or no re-experiencing of group association. As a matter of fact, it is a new experience for many of the participants. It may in certain cases such as that of a person long retired, bring renewed recognition of status to one or more members of the family. It usually brings out in greater simplicity the purposes and ideals to which the person devoted his public life.

Theory of the Functioning of Funerals. A concise statement of the principles governing the influence of the funeral on the family, the group and the community is given below to bring into perspective the points that have been made at greater length in this chapter. It will serve to make clearer the measure in which the stimulus for the funeral operates in various situations, and the social factors that limit the significance of funerals. It will serve also to lay the foundation for the treatment of the effect of death and the funeral on the individual, to be given in a later chapter.

It is the sense of interruption that provides the stimulus to hold the funeral, interruption of the interaction of individuals within the family, or within a group, or interruption of activity of the whole community. The larger the group or the community, the less actual interruption occurs because of the loss of a member. The more intimate, continuous and vital the interaction between the individuals has been, and the more the group activity has been regarded as vital to the welfare of the members, the greater the need to provide for some sort of group experience to bring about a new equilibrium.

This need is met by a repitition of group association at a meeting in which the social aspect is the predominant feature. On a higher level the need for reassurance is met in a ritual at which the group contemplates the common underlying ideals of the society, as well as philosophical and spiritual assurance that life is worth while. In the degree to which the death has disturbed interaction or activity will the disturbance shift the concern of those affected from the habitual prosecution of daily tasks to the problem of reestablishing reliance both on the beneficent working of the community or society, and on its guiding principles.

On the family of the deceased devolves the responsibility to carry through a series of gatherings providing the community with the means of reassuring itself. The family is hard pressed and distraught, and needs the sense of a supportive community around it. From this feeling arises an enhanced desire to be regarded in the community as worthy of sympathy, and hence the family seeks from the funeral a heightened status.

The three social effects to be hoped for of the funeral, a sense of solidarty in the group, reassurance of the validity of the ideals and guiding principles commonly accepted, and a heightened rapport of the family with the community, are actually realized when the community of interacting individuals is small enough in numbers and coherent enough for the individuals in it to know each other.

The question that obtrudes itself, in view of the foregoing analysis is: what factors prevent a fuller functioning of the modern funeral, especially in urban areas? There are three partial answers. First, for a re-experiencing of group association and a consequent augmenting of group solidarity, it is essential that the dead person should have been an integral part of an interacting number of individuals. That situation is found only in small measures, if association with all the residents of a city neighborhood, or association with one group of persons in all activities, is meant. The growing multiplicity of organizations in modern urban society has steadily whittled away the significance of the funeral.

A second partial answer to the question concerning the lack of significance of many funerals lies both in the diversity of ideals held by various segments of the population and in the impoverishment of social ideals in a changing society.

The third answer to the fundamental question lies in the relation of the family to the rest of the community. It is the members of the family who act for the deceased at the funeral; it is they who appeal through the wake and the religious service for public recognition of his life and accomplishments. When the family is connected only with a number of unrelated organizations and with a widespread net of casual individual acquaintances, there exists no practical opportunity to make an effective appeal for recognition. Even if all the connections of a person could be brought together, there frequently is no one basis in the moral, ethical or spiritual areas, on which to make an appeal. As a consequence, in many funerals the family accepts "an ounce of dross for its ounce of gold," and pours out its longing for recognition in extravagant display.

A bitter deduction from this line of thought could be drawn, namely, that the death of one person is not so important as once it would have been, at least to the community in which he has lived. To state the conclusion is almost to refute it; for the death of any one represents a universal tragedy only made more dreadful by the growth of population. The trouble lies in the persistent effort to make the old form of the funeral serve in a situation in which it functions poorly. There is as great a need as ever for a recognition of the sorrows of bereavement; there is even greater need for unity on basic values and high ideals for this generation. Individuals, groups and communities cannot afford to ignore the stimulus that arises from a death to assay the kinds and amount of vital interaction between persons and groups, nor the incentive to get a perspective on the lives of close associates, and through it a deeper understanding of the meaning of their own lives.

(For an outline of analyses of funerals among simpler peoples, see Appendix V).

CHAPTER XI

TRENDS AND EXPERIMENTS

Discontent is the first step in the progress of a man or nation.

OSCAR WILDE

The need of fundamental changes in the conduct of the funeral is shown by developments in family and community life in the last few generations and by the widespread dissatisfaction with present procedures. Little has been done by the industry itself. There are, however, certain trends in the industry and several organized experimental projects going on, an understanding of which will lead up to any further proposals that may seem to grow out of the findings of the present study. They will be briefly outlined in this chapter after a glimpse into the long range character of the dissatisfaction with the funeral.

The Long-Felt Need For Change. Funerals have changed in the direction of elaboration and fleeting elegance, but the fundamental criticisms of them have been the same for many decades. In 1930, long after embalming and motorized transportation equipment became common, a famous settlement worker, Graham Taylor, a man of keen social vision and with a heart of unusual sympathy and understanding, wrote of conditions among the poor in Chicago, as follows:

"The pathos of these funeral customs is that most frequently they are the one and only distinction of the whole life, and yet are conferred after death. . . . Pride, display and indiscriminating honor heedlessly bestowed upon the best and worst—the most spectacular scenes often attending the burial of the worst—are indeed to be deplored.

"The living need protection from being sacrificed for the dead by the extravagant indulgence of their own grief, as well as by the exactions of custom, the pride of benefit orders, and by the wasteful if not extortionate toll laid upon the bereaved by unscrupulous funeral trades. . . . Frequently nothing is left to meet the immediate needs of the widow and dependent children." (1, pp. 197, 198).

It is both sad and irritating to realize that much the same thing bas been said before and after Taylor's time by many settlement

workers.   Going back almost sixty years, to the monologue of a character through which Mark Twain spoke, the same sort of indictment
is brought against funeral practices.

"The adoption of cremation would relieve us of much of threadbare
burial witticisms; but on the other hand, it would resurrect a lot of
mildewed old cremation-jokes that have had a rest for two thousand
years.

"I have a colored acquaintance who . . . never earns above four
hundred dollars a year . . . he has a wife and several young children. . . .   To such a man a funeral is a colossal financial disaster. . . .
This man lost a little child. . . .   He bought the cheapest (coffin) he
could find, plain wood, stained.   It cost him *twenty six dollars*.   It
would have cost less than four, probably, if it had been built to put
something useful into.

An alleged undertaker puts the situation this way:

"There's one thing in this world which a person don't say—'I'll look
around a little, and if I can't do better, I'll come back and take it!'
That's a coffin.   And take your poor man, and if you work him right
he'll bust himself on a single lay out.   Or especially a woman.

". . . in ordinary times, a person dies, and we lay him up on ice;
one day, two days, maybe three, to wait for friends to come.   Takes a
lot of it—melts fast.   We charge jewelry rates for that ice, and war
prices for attendance.   Well, don't you know, when there's an epidemic, they rush 'em to the cemetery the minute the breath's out.
No market for ice in an epidemic.   Same with embalming.   You take
a family that's able to embalm, and you've got a soft thing. . . .   It's
human nature—human nature in grief.   It don't reason you see."
(2, pp. 304, 308)

The problem is acute, and of long standing. Change is overdue.

Trend Toward Larger Establishments Within the Industry.   The
trend within the funeral industry toward larger, more efficient establishments may, in time, bring about a reduction in the number of
practitioners, and thereby a lessening of the pressure on the remaining firms to get from each client the maximum possible financial
return.   In larger, more active establishments less cost per case may
be involved since plant, equipment, and personnel can be utilized to
capacity.   It is possible that more business-like attitudes might supersede high pressure practices.   Little change in that direction is observable at present, however, in the firms affiliated with the groups
leading in the direction spoken of, namely, the National Selected

Morticians, the Advertising Funeral Directors Association, and the individual chains and mergers.

There is slight indication that another trend favorable to the consumer may be taking place. This is a strengthening of a sense of security on the part of the successful funeral director-proprietor. Since status in the business increases with volume, investment and amount of profit, the successful operators may become less prone to defenses and pretentions in the future. The same end may be partly brought about, by the fact that his association with dead bodies is less direct and any aversion to him felt by others on that score is lessened or obviated. On the other hand, the power of undertakers grows with the increase of wealth and standing of individuals. As a result, lobbying influence may become even more potent than at present if the undertaking industry is dominated by a group of very successful operators. Merging may in time approximate monopoly, accompanied by arbitrary price setting outside the bargaining context altogether, and the consumer's interests may then rest in the lap of the financial gods.

Public Enterprise, Cooperatives and Labor Plans. Discontent over mortuary practices, especially in the face of long continued failure of the industry itself to eliminate exploitation among some of its members, has stimulated recurring demands for other forms of control. That the business does not operate according to the laws of supply and demand, or of price structure and the elimination of submarginal operators, furnishes further cause to look to means other than these laws to eliminate abuses, and to bring costs of funeral services within the means of bereaved families. Public enterprise frequently is suggested as the answer. It is made more plausible by the need for large scale standardization and operation, a process that is being demonstrated by a few groups within the industry.

A demand for such relief from the high costs of funerals was made in 1921 by a clergyman, Quincy L. Dowd, who had been aroused by the privations he saw families undergo in order to pay the undertaker. His book reports a study of state and municipal provisions for burials and funeral management abroad, where public provisions have long been made and public services operated successfully. (3).

One form the demand takes, following the pattern of certain European countries, is to make funeral service a public utility subject to public utility regulations, a demand appearing occasionally in a state legislature. Another related proposal, offered for each of several years in the New York State Legislature, provides permission for the creation of municipal funeral authorities in large cities. A bill embodying the proposal in New York State offered a carefully worked out plan for the erection and equipment of a municipal funeral plant at a cost of $920,000 on a self liquidating basis. The claim was made that a funeral then costing $300 could be given by such a municipal authority for between sixty and seventy dollars. The lobbies representing funeral interests have effectively opposed efforts of the kind. The opposition to such proposals is based primarily on the unsubstantiated argument that the service would be of low grade and that "people would not stand for it."

To bring the conduct of funerals under social control and at the same time to avoid official investment and direction, the suggestion has been made that a limited dividend corporation headed by a philanthropic citizen, be formed to market funerals and funeral paraphernalia at prices within the reach of the majority of the population.

The high prices of funerals throughout the country, the methods used by undertakers, and the ornate style urged on clients, all stand as a perennial invitation to consumers to take the service into their own hands and to maintain it under their own control. The invitation has been accepted by a relative few, largely farmers. The cooperative funeral associations maintained by them are, for the most part, an outgrowth of the larger cooperative movement. Figures for 1950, quoted by the U. S. Department of Labor in the *Monthly Labor Review* of October, 1951, show a total of 28 associations furnishing complete funerals. 23 of them are farm groups; 3 furnishing caskets only; and 8 furnishing burials on contract with funeral establishments. The combined membership amounts to nearly 55,000, in 39 societies. Many of the societies are located in the West North Central area. The majority of them are federated in state associations.

These cooperatives are well established, although their recent development has been slow. Economically they have succeeded, saving their members on an average $150 to $200 per funeral, calculated on prices prevailing in their localities. Each organization, is society owned, having a mortuary establishment, and following the seven principles of the Rochdale cooperative movement. Except for the societies which furnish funerals on contract, and those furnishing caskets only, each group engages its own funeral director. The great achievements to the credit of the cooperative funeral associations consist, first, of the altered relationship between the bereaved family and the funeral director. The latter is entirely service minded since no profit is involved in the transaction. Further, the services are rendered by the employee of the members themselves, and any margin between costs and charges is returned to the members in the form of patronage dividends.

The achievements consist, secondly, in conformity of the style of the funeral to the client's manner of living. There is no urging to choose an ostentatious casket or elaborate accessories. Further, since there is more homogeneity in the group of members than in the clientele of the profit enterprise, especially in the matter of economic status, the incentive to make a glamorous showing is minimal. There is often something of a group spirit engendered in the democratic organizational activities and control of cooperatives, and it tends to make funeral observances more socially significant.

An extension of cooperative funeral associations is advocated by the National Council of Churches, the Cooperative League of the U.S.A. and by many labor and liberal groups. The cooperatives are belittled publicly at every turn by the large funeral directors associations. Laws in most states have been enacted which prohibit a corporation from selling "professional" services to the general public. This brings into question the relation of the cooperative funeral association to the services of its manager. Lack of precedent and in some states laws stand in the way of granting incorporation papers to a cooperative.

Private profit undertakers' lobbies create difficulties for the establishment of the non profit groups. (4), (5, p. 12). In one large eastern state the undertakers have been able to gain a tight monopoly. No new undertakers' licenses were issued by the state at the time a cooperative funeral society was in the making. Pressure was brought against the selling of a license to the cooperative by those who otherwise might have been willing to do so. As a result the only cooperative activity possible has been a funeral advisory service rendered by an existing consumers cooperative society. In certain communities the organization of a cooperative funeral society has brought upon its members adverse criticism from various local sources inspired by fear of competition. In addition to these difficulties, the high cost of construction has been a hindrance to the expansion of funeral cooperatives.

The great social service of the cooperatives has been to demonstrate the feasibility of consumer organization and the possibility of furnishing adequate and satisfying funerals at moderate costs.

Organized labor in two conspicuous instances has taken over the "unpleasant" task, as it calls it, of the negotiations between families that have been bereaved and funeral directors. It has applied to them and to the undertaker the principles it has followed in collective bargaining with employers. The example of the cooperative funeral societies has helped them to crystallize a pattern of procedure. The greatest stimulus has been the long-felt exactions of the funeral directors from working families devoid of financial surplus to meet high burial costs. In addition, however, the exploitation of a whole community in time of disaster served as a sharp spur to organized effort. Immediately following the Centralia, Illinois mine disaster, the families were charged an average of $732 a funeral.

In the journal of the U. A. W. - C. I. O., in 1950, the announcement appeared that the welfare committee of the union would furnish members with information concerning burial allowances to which they were entitled from the Veterans Administration or from Social Security. An agreement was worked out between the Motor City Coop and a funeral director which provided "dignified funerals at about half the cost of a free enterprise funeral." (6, p. 7) (7, p. 25). In St. Louis, the organizing committee represented both A. F. of L. and C. I. O. unions with a total of 60,000 member families, who were brought into a similar arrangement with equally satisfying results.

The possibilities of the development of funeral projects in the large unified labor movement are great. It remains a lively possibility whenever less than prosperous times make the cost of ornate funerals intolerable to workers. The most significant features of the plan of these two labor groups are the realization on the part of their leaders of the folly of expensive display at funerals, and the advocacy within the labor movement of moderate expenditures.

Church Funeral Societies. The efforts for public, cooperative, and labor-group control over funerals have sprung primarily from the economic motive. Other organized deviations have arisen only in part out of the repugnance to wasteful spending.

The dissatisfaction of many churches with the usual conduct of funerals was described in Chapter VI. It has taken organized expression in a number of funeral or memorial societies affiliated with, and usually staffed by, the church workers or church volunteers. Typically, when individuals or families join such a society they indicate their preferences for type of body disposal, choice of funeral director, and selection of type of funeral or memorial service. The society comes to an agreement with one or more funeral directors who are willing to give their services at moderate rates in exchange for the assurance of obtaining a number of funerals which they otherwise could not expect to get.

Advantage for the consumer consists, first, in the strength that comes to him in the bargaining process when his representative speaks for many clients; second, in the opportunity to avoid the personal experience of bargaining which to many is unpleasant, and to put the responsibility on the representative of the society. For the client and the church the arrangement makes for a procedure at the funeral or memorial services which conflicts least with the mortician. Church funeral societies emphasize simplicity and inexpensiveness, artistic use of flowers, contributions to good causes instead of the usual gifts of floral pieces, increasing use of cremation, memorial services to be held on a date when relatives and friends can attend, preferably in the church, shunning of the lugubrious and morbid, and discouragement of embalming and "viewing."

More than in any other group, church societies are to be found in association with Unitarian churches in all sections of the country. Fewer of them have been organized by Universalist churches. The Friends Meeting in Yellow Springs, Ohio has instituted a plan of disposal involving the use of the unpaid services of a committee of friends of the deceased, who lay out the body, arrange the necessary legal and business details, and convey the body to the crematorium. Appropriate memorial services are held later in accordance with the wishes of the family.

Church funeral societies have satisfied those who have patronized them. However they have never reached any high degree of organization. The potential service they could render is almost limitless. There is no reason why most of them should serve largely the members of a single institution since the pattern on which they are organized involves service to any one who joins. There has been little aggressive effort to extend their benefits, due primarily to two factors. First, Protestant churches are independent and individualistic, and extensive cooperative effort between them seldom occurs. The second factor is the failure to put continuous effort into promotion.

The administration of the society's business is all too often left by the minister and top lay leadership to a member of the staff as one

more added responsibility.   The efforts of labor unions and of churches
seldom, if ever, are joined.   Possibly a further limitation of the church
societies has occasionally operated to restrict their usefulness, namely
the narrow area of information they furnish for their members.   Guidance is sometimes needed by the family on matters of public assistance, such as Social Security and Veterans' benefits, and on procedures
for the gift of eyes (See Appendix I), or of the body for scientific purposes.   (See Appendix II)

Whereas burial is provided for universally among the societies, cremation is usually emphasized, particularly where crematoria are within reasonable distance.   Except for those faiths in which cremation is
contrary to religious doctrine, it provides a device that may be utilized
at little expense through which the memorial service can be set at any
time.   The pressure of time on the family is thereby greatly relieved.
(See Appendix III).

Secular Gatherings, Family, Group and Testimonial Meetings.   The
tradition of the funeral as necessarily a function of the church or
synagogue is strong in the United States, and holds even for some
persons who have lost their identity with any religious body.   When
the influence of the institution of religion ramified into every phase of
social relations, the final obsequies in church fairly represented the
totality of the life of the deceased and the interests of his survivors.
Today, however, it is not the all embracing institution that it once was;
for some persons the closest associations lie outside the church.   At
the death of such a person his relatives and friends want to pay their
last respects to him in surroundings that remind them of associations
with him during his life time.

These small gatherings are not a new phenomenon; they represent
either an alternative to the more religious service, or an additional
meeting to provide a renewal of intimate association.   They are a very
adaptable device, particularly in an urban situation in which for many
the traditional funeral seems to have lost much of its significance.   The
same pattern is followed sometimes by the leaders of an organization
when one of their prominent members has died.   A meeting is called as
a memorial to the dead, usually after the remains have been buried or
cremated, but sometimes in the presence of the casket.   The meeting
is apt to take the form of other organization sessions, with the usual
leadership in charge.   There is no sharp dividing line between such
informal gatherings and the funeral conducted by a fraternal order or
a patriotic society and the funeral service in a liberal church.   At any

of them speeches may be made by representatives of organizations to which the deceased belonged. Colleagues at colleges or universities have sometimes organized very informally and arranged to speak at a small gathering whenever one of them dies.

In the types of gatherings described above there is a tendency among less religiously inclined groups to take the conduct of the funeral service into their own hands. Another phenomenon in the United States bears no relation to the funeral but performs certain of its functions. It is the testimonial dinner, or the meeting to present an award to honor an individual.

The similarity of the funeral and the testimonial meeting, is often referred to jokingly by the person being honored. Actually the testimonial gathering, when analyzed from the point of view assumed in Chapter X, does produce much the same results: (1) an enhancement of group feeling on the part of those who know or follow the honored guest; (2) a rededication to the ideals or the movement he represents; and (3) a sharper realization of his status. The testimonial meeting, however, brings prestige to the honored individual and focuses less attention on the family. The testimonial dinner brings out a larger attendance than the funeral, except in those cultural groups in which the funeral is the great occasion on which to demonstrate solidarity. The dinner can be planned, organized, and advertised for weeks in advance, avoiding the time pressure felt at funerals. Costs are laid, not on the family but on the guests.

Display is shared by all, in the elegance of the room in which the dinner is held, in the garb of the diners and in the service of the waiters. Solemnity, while too often a feature of the speeches, is not obligatory, while the exaggerations of praise are worse than eulogies at funerals. Testimonial meetings fit the needs of large city populations better than do funerals. For one thing they serve to bring more sharply into focus the ramifications of the life of the honored guest. The emphasis on the individual fits into the social structure of the city where the family carries less weight than in small communities and the individual is recognized more on his personal merits. Lastly, testimonial meetings serve a social function most effectively in the case of the prominent person.

Bequest of Eyes or Body For Medical Purposes. The individual ordinarily can look forward to his death with a reasonable certitude that his body will become an obligation, a burden, and an expense to his nearest relative. Yet few ever concern themselves with the possibility of making arrangements to render their bodies useful to society, and less or no burden to those nearest them. The fact that caring for the dead body is a task so peripheral to the daily functioning of the community is undoubtedly one factor responsible for the general obtuseness in this regard. For the members of the very few religious bodies in which burial of the body intact is essential, there is, of course, no possibility of any other disposition of it. Since the pronouncement of Pope Pius XII on May 14, 1956, Roman Catholics are at full liberty to have corneas from the eyes of the dead transplanted to those of the living. One other factor is involved, namely, the failure to dissociate quickly the affection for the person from the bodily remains.

At the same time it is apparent that medical science has been one of the few greatest benefactors of mankind. Practically all persons honored at funerals have benefited by that science. Yet at their deaths there occurs the destruction of two of the most necessary means of alleviating suffering and aiding in the acquisition of skill by the physician and surgeon of tomorrow. Throughout the country medical schools need cadavers for the pursuit of anatomical studies. Twenty thousand blind persons need the corneal tissue from the eyes of fellow humans who have died. These unseeing persons could see if they could benefit by the eyes of young persons or old, of those who used glasses or those who did not.

The greatest obstacle to the dedication of the eyes or the body for socially useful purposes is the lack of knowledge on the part of the responsible person in charge of funeral arrangements of the procedure to follow. Accurate acquaintance with the precise steps to be followed when death occurs should be acquired beforehand, and certain arrangements made to give eyes or body. (See Appendices I and II

When it is desired to have the remains taken by a medical college, the prospective donor should get in touch with one or more schools near his residence to be sure that one of them accepts bodies. He should make out a statement (an affidavit) stating his wish, and have it witnessed and retained by his spouse or next of kin. That person also makes out a statement that is witnessed, saying that he or she agrees to turning over of the body to the medical school. When death occurs, the certificate of death should be secured and the medical school notified immediately to come and get the body. The school's representative will secure the burial permit and register the death and disposition of the body at the office of the health department. (See Appendix II).

To bequeath eyes to the Eye-Bank, a prospective donor should get in touch with the Eye-Bank for Sight Restoration, Incorporated, long before death is expected. A form for release of the corneal tissue will be sent by the Eye-Bank and instructions to be kept and followed implicitly by the spouse or next of kin when the donor dies.

The donor should fill out the release sent by the Eye-Bank and see to it that his spouse or next of kin carefully keeps it for use when death occurs. More than 170 of the nation's leading hospitals, the chief depositors with the Eye-Bank, rush any available eyes by the Red Cross Motor Corps or via air line to the main headquarters to the Eye-Bank. There "doctors and laboratory men make complete pathological examinations of the eyes, attend to their preservation, and if the corneas are perfect for grafting, distribute them in turn to qualified surgeons throughout the country with suitable cases. A surgeon is told when his turn is next and informs the first patient on his list, who, with pounding heart, answers the call to rush to the hospital—the call that may well mean he will see again." (8, p. 10).

PART IV

OVERVIEW

CHAPTER XII

MEANINGS AND MEANINGFUL FUNERALS

Not tame and gentle bliss, but disaster, heroically encountered, is
man's true happy ending.
LEWIS MUMFORD

The soul that is opening, and before whose eyes material objects
vanish, is lost in sheer joy.
HENRI BERGSON

Thus far in this study the funeral has been looked at from several
angles. It is necessary now to see it whole in the light that is focused
on it. The findings of previous chapters will be utilized, not so much
to review them as to create a composite picture. The dominating purpose up to this point has been to find facts and apply logic to them:
my logic, if you will, but logic as devoid of bias as human nature would
allow. Purposes of my own undoubtedly have sneaked in to some of
the interpretations, but the plan and intent have envisaged only critical
analysis.

The present chapter will present further factual material but will
be in part more subjective than the ones preceding. Hence the reader
is expected to begin this chapter with his own critical faculties actively
operating. He is expected to come to judgments of his own. I am
providing a token set of deductions and inferences.

As one looks over the mass of observations, explanations, and interpretations of funeral activities and relationships, certain generalizations appear. They seem to play upon each other. The various
happenings cluster around threads of interpretation, which seem to
weave themselves into a pattern of relationships between the principal
actors. Out of the effort to interweave interpretations, some value
judgments must arise: either the funeral is useless today, or it has
unique values in it. If there are values to be realized more fully by
observing funerals, then what are they, and what criteria do they sug-

140

gest for a program that will fit the needs of individuals and groups in an urban, segmented society?

Insight by the Bereaved Into Ultimate Ends. Many persons state that there has been for them a value in the funeral that meets one of the two greatest needs of the associates of the dead. It is a value peculiar to the funeral because of the unique effect of death upon the living who have met sorrow because of it. In an urban society people live close to death, occurring daily around or near them, but seldom met face to face. When it does come to a loved one, its shock is greater because it has been unforeseen and unprepared for.

Grief that is suffered by the bereaved members of the family or by close friends is an affliction that remains with the sufferer for months or years, only gradually lessening and disappearing. The funeral helps the grieving persons in three principal ways: first through the solace that comes from sympathetic friends, second from the comfort that promises of religion afford, and third through the help often found by the individual in the funeral to overcome the shock to his own assurance in the basic assumptions underlying his personal activities. It is one of the ironies of human development that change for the better often cannot be effected, nor the need for it realized, until frustration and serious unhappiness are encountered.

With the frustration of response from the one who has died, those closest to him experience a keen consciousness not only of their loss, but of the meaning of life itself. Death induces one to hold up a mirror to life, to see in perspective the trivia of daily living, and the ultimate ends for which routine tasks are performed.

The experience is one of the rare events in a lifetime when all values are thrown on a screen in their entirety, and the whole meaning of life is poignantly present. The worth whileness of living is at stake in the manner and thoroughness with which the individual meets the issue. Inseparably bound up with the worthiness to him of living is the worth of himself in his own estimation. To evade the clear challenge is to admit oneself incapable of fulfilling the unique place ascribed to man by scientists and prophets. To accept it is to take the first step toward a renewed, and possibly an ennobled life. (15, pp. 132-135)

Moments of this kind are invaluable in the ordering of lives to reach their greatest possibilities. It is therefore of the utmost importance that the individuals experiencing them be given every help in exploring the ideals for which they have lived, and in reaffirming or reorganizing the hierarchy of values by which they intend to live. This is

no time for escape into the tawdriness of funeral display. The ceremony is primarily a highlighted opportunity in the period following
the death for each participant to call on himself to make severe judgments on his own life's loyalties and work, and to make his own "re-
joinder to the experiences of life."   (1), (2).

The minds of those bereaved by death turn spontaneously not only
to the ultimate ends for which they live and strive, but also to the
riddle of the continuity of individual existence. The inexorable passage of time and the consequent limitations on the achievements of the
individual, present themselves in vivid reality, and demand fundamental reconciliation with the deep desire to persist indefinitely. Traditionally, because of the concern of the bereaved over this frustrating
characteristic of all life, stress has been laid on family history and on
the continuity of generations.

One consolation dwelt upon by clergy of all faiths and by the leaders
of rationalistic thinking, is a sense of the place of man in the long
stretches of time: a perspective of evolving stages of the cosmos and
the evolutionary process as it includes man. Wonderment, possible at
all times for anyone who contemplates the age long development of the
race, becomes an active force at the time when death has occurred
close by. And with it comes almost universally a profound feeling of
humility in a world of driving competition. There is also deepened
appreciation of tradition that comes with the perspective of time to a
person living in an era of rapid technological and social change.

A third aspect of the yearning normally stimulated in the heart and
mind of the bereaved person is the need of assurance that personal and
family social relations hold as strongly as ever. Some persons describe
the gripping experience as one of being suddenly and utterly alone,
while looking straight into the great unknown. The overwhelming
craving for a renewed and deepened sense of companionship and affection lies at the root of the wake. In the inmost consciousness of the
sorrowing individual it is an integral part of a longing which includes
anxiety about the ideals he cherishes and the craving for persistence
of the self.

In home, school and group life these aims have been formed, nur-
tured and maintained. The consciousness of self and its purposes has
arisen in social interaction; and when the inevitable end of one's own
life is fore-shadowed by the termination of another, then anxious concern arises for assurance that the fostering relations of kinship and
friendship will continue as long as one shall live.

The full consciousness of the promises which religious faiths offer comes critically essential at this time. So also is needed assurance of exerting a continuing influence in the world through the lives of ones children or the influence one has on other lives. Identification with an enduring worldly cause to which one can give service and loyalty during his life time is essential if he is later to make his most fruitful contributions in home, community and society.

The chief characteristic of the desire for an inner consciousness of fellowship on the part of the persons who feel it most keenly, is the sense of equality among friends. The craving is for acceptance of themselves without reservation as well as for the uninhibited giving of affection. The scramble for status seems to be foreign to the quality of feeling that is experienced.

The three aspects of the need of a bereaved person are all of one piece; they represent three phases of the desire for assurance that he is worth-while and that his life counts. At the moment when he sees another life snuffed out, he wants to know that he is secure in the matters that are most profoundly and lastingly significant; that in the vast expanse of time his existence has its place; that in the realm of the highest ethical and religious values his strivings play their part; and that among his fellows he is a loved and needed individual.

The experience just described in its threefold dimensions is compounded of instinctive desire, strong feeling, and an exercise of the intellectual faculties. That it is partly imaginative or intuitive is patently true, but that it is therefore unreal or impractical is strictly untrue. It is akin to what Albert Schweitzer has called elemental thinking: that which starts from the fundamental questions about the relations of man to the universe, about the meanings of life, and about the nature of goodness. John Dewey linked the trio of basic considerations, if not explicitly, at least in clear inference: "The things in civilization we most prize . . . exist by the grace of the doings and sufferings of the continuous human community in which we are a link. Ours is the responsibility of conserving, transmitting, rectifying and expanding the values we have received that those who come after us may receive it more solid and secure, more widely accessible and more generously shared than we have received it." (3, p. 87).

To help the human spirit vitally to realize its role in the realms of time, of values, and the living community is to help it to adjust to the reality of death. Death so accepted brings no guilt; it is seen as a part of life itself. In fact, the experience for many has been one of achievement. It has brought to them a new configuration of their own values and a perspective of the relation of life and death. It is an experience of "heroically encountering" the threat of the last disaster, and by facing it realistically, of gaining a vivid sense of triumph over it. It comes with differing force to different persons, and its reality cannot be questioned.

The fundamental needs of the individual aroused by the thought of dying are the obverse of the social functions described in Chapter X. They are two sides of the same thing. As the individual, facing the inexorable fact that his life on earth is not everlasting turns to the assurances that his influence will continue, so the funeral group, permeated with the sense of its own weaknesses and destructibility turns to the assurances that come with the re-experiencing of group association, giving to each other something of the same ability to "go on" as it gives to the bereaved members within it.

In so doing it helps to reaffirm its own solidarity, answering another of the three cravings of the individual, namely, to be accepted and loved by his fellow men when a death has drawn aside for a moment the curtains shutting out the vast loneliness of the unknown. The individual reaches out for companionship; the group most disturbed by the death, the family, seeks desperately in answer to a like need, to gain the acceptance and approval of the community.

And as the individual spontaneously finds worth in his life through his identification with the ideals and the intangible excellencies of the good life, so the group looks to the purposes of its foundation, to the high values underlying the machinery of its day to day aspiration, rather than to the details of carrying out the group purposes.

Clouded Values and Insulated Relations. The three attributes of the deep concern of the bereaved person, namely, emphasis on the fundamental ideals and purposes in life, craving for a sense of close association with relatives and friends, and anxiety about the persistence of self—these are all recognized by almost every religion. They are, in fact, three of the most universal and enduring of the concerns of every faith. At the time of the funeral those most affected by the death are thinking and feeling on the level of deepest social, ethical and spiritual values. It would follow that on that same level the funeral should serve the needs of those participating in it. It is anomalous that tawdry materialistic features characterize many funerals. How can they be explained? Why have the occasions of assemblage at so vital a crisis lessened in importance in recent decades?

The trouble lies basically in the failure of the culture to hold up clear and authoritative norms or ideals. The need of individuals for them is the same as in former generations, and probably will be much the same in the future.

The answers to the needs have become clouded; the kind and quality of thinking and feeling to meet the crisis of death in the family have slipped into the background of consciousness. Nevertheless they are still to be found if sought, although they are easily neglected in the shift of attention to new and more tangible matters. This is an era of hectic effort to understand the continuing wonders of science and technology. Accompanying this effort is a casual reliance on an automatic preservation of the deeper values. It is an era of transitional and confused beliefs and half acknowledged doubts.

There is no unifying center to the culture, and hence no place or occasion on which convincing and unquestioned answers to cultural needs can be enunciated. (5, pp. 20, 21) Expressions of profound values sound hollow in the ears of a large number of people.

It is therefore an acceptable thing at many funerals to relegate all vital anxieties to the minimal period of church attendance and to succumb to the practice of conspicuous consumption devised by the undertakers. Few people clearly understand either their own feelings or the necessary inner processes through which can be secured deep satisfaction and a fortified determination to "go on." The realization of the need to consider one's hierarchy of values comes seldom, and faintly, in the course of vocational and leisure time activities. Social amenities on the whole become pressures to conform to a superficial way of thinking and behaving. When, then, death does occur and the yearnings described above are felt the easiest thing to do is to suppress or ignore them. To acknowledge and face them seems to many to be outmodedly sentimental or touched with unfashionable mysticism. To face them is terrifying to some.

"Our own era simply denies death and with it one fundamental aspect of life. Instead of allowing the awareness of death and suffering to become one of the strongest incentives for life, the basis for human solidarity, and an experience without which joy and enthusiasm lack intensity and depth, the individual is forced to repress it. But, as is always the case with repression, by being removed from sight the repressed elements do not cease to exist. Thus the fear of death lives an illegitimate existence among us. It remains alive in spite of the attempt to deny it, but being repressed it remains sterile. It is one source of the flatness of other experiences, of the restlessness pervading life, and it explains, I would venture to say, the exorbitant amount of money this nation pays for its funerals." (6, pp. 245, 246).

Many of the strains felt at funeral assemblages are due in the last analysis to the failure of the current patterns of behavior to give expression to the emotional needs and intellectual frustration of those who have experienced closest relations to the deceased.

We have seen that the culture of modern America is not conducive to meeting the need of the bereaved individual for a clarification of fundamental life purposes at the typical funeral. The need for a strengthening of the sense of companionship and social solidarity is answered only in part for another reason. It is the inadequacy of the funeral to reach into the various areas of the social relations of the deceased. Such failure results in a very partial and superficial answer to the individual's great need to feel that life is whole so far as human connections go.

The general framework of the funeral as it is known today, grew up over a long, historic period in which the intimate institutions to which people belonged could be encompassed in a small geographical area. The home, the job, the church, and the school were close together. Hence visiting the family after a death could be done by associates in all realms of activity. The church service satisfied the need to see and feel camaraderie with all the close friends and colleagues of the deceased. Or, to put the matter in terms of the functions of the funeral; since the norms of the community encompassed the ideals of all its sectors; the family found its place in the community reaffirmed; and the coming together in the wake was a re-experiencing of a totality of group experiences.

The desire of the bereaved person for sympathetic insight into all the areas of activity of the deceased is just as great today. But the family, the job, the church, and the fraternal groupings are centers of differing groups. The social world of the one who has died is a number of relatively disparate structures. There is no central point at which they meet, no all-inclusive community of understanding, no comprehensively sympathetic relationships. The individual contemplating the death of a friend or relative often is at a loss to see connection between the social groups to which the deceased belonged.

Essential Elements of Meaningful Funerals. The temporal and commercial aspects of the typical funeral are unsuited to the needs of the individual, the family and the community. Intelligent speculation on the features of a funeral which would meet the present needs must begin with a realization of the defects of current practices as they have been outlined in previous chapters. Categorically stated, they are as follows:

1. The leadership and virtual control of all but the clergyman's part (now in the hands of an efficiently operating group of men under abnormal pressure to induce lavish expenditures) needs to be transferred to influences that are social and professional.

2. The technical and materialistic features of the funeral need to be made completely subordinate to the psychological, social and spiritual aspects.

3. The inordinate emphasis on the body and the mechanisms to adorn it and keep it above ground, need to give way to sensible and satisfying methods of disposing of it.

4. The enormous, cruel and unnecessary costs of funerals to families, as well as the burden of culturally determined responsibilities that put the family under intolerable and inescapable obligations, must be drastically reduced.

5. The family, which is at great disadvantage in it negotiations with the funeral establishment, needs to be strengthened by institutional and collective action.

6. The procedures following a death need to be geared into the operations of the functioning community and brought back from the shadowy, tangential status they now occupy.

7. Funeral practices should become an integral part of all the institutional efforts to develop maturity and self control in every individual.

8. When a death occurs the focus of thought and feeling of everyone concerned should be on the enhancement of life's values for the living.

It is impossible by mere logic to persuade people to make radical departures from custom and tradition. Measures to be proposed in the following paragraphs fall within the range of change that appears feasible. They are quite in consonance with the cultural prescriptions. and are flexible enough to allow for differences between ethnic and religious groups. The suggested modifications are not innovations in any absolute sense. All have been put into practice and have been proved successful in limited measure. One purpose of the presently proposed changes is to make possible the fulfillment of any deeply imbedded cultural compulsions while affording an answer to individual and social needs in the modern community. Another purpose is to make possible a significant observance of the demise of a friend or relative by the considerable minority for whom the traditional funeral holds little or no meaning.

The important human consideration concerning funerals is their meaningfulness to the participants, particularly to those most deeply affected by the death. To hold gatherings merely because of a weak tradition is not only mummery; it is also a mockery that compounds the tragedy which has struck the family and closest friends. Any constructive action on the problem of funerals then must be centered on their significance to the individuals involved and also to their communities. It is therefore to the problem of expressing meanings within the practical situation of today that the last words of this study of funerals are addressed.

The first essential of the funeral, in all but the ritual of the church, is that it have unique meaning to the family and close friends. It should take the form they desire, and hence should be planned by them. Certain of its features will follow the pattern of the faith professed by the deceased. Other features may or may not be traditional, according to the wishes of those most concerned. The life, affections, and work of the honored dead form for most persons the basis of their wishes for a farewell to him. The uniformity of present usage should give way to individually adapted procedures, whatever they may be.

Active, purposeful planning by those who have been closest to the deceased should supersede the passive acceptance of a pattern devised by individuals outside the circle of close associates. The function of the funeral director should consist of finding the technical means of carrying out the self determined wishes of the family. The wake, especially, should take the form of a gathering planned as a social affair that will be expressive of one man's interests, associates, and manner of living. The formal, especially the funereal features of the wake, should be eliminated. Only by so doing can the occasion be made to serve the needs of the mourners or the community. That it be held at all, or that it should be a matter of open house for a number of occasions, should not be obligatory. More than one gathering for more than one circle of friends or associates would be completely acceptable from the standpoint of propriety.

The order of precedence of the gatherings in the funeral period should also be regarded as a flexible matter. There is no valid reason why the religious ceremony should terminate the observance of the death. There are many instances in which the friendly social atmosphere of the wake is more appropriate after the religious service. This is true when the service has been a memorial gathering from which the body or ashes are absent. From the standpoint of the experience of many families, and from that of abstract theory, any re-experiencing of group association would operate most effectively as a final stage in the funeral proceedings. The frequent spontaneous activity of relatives, friends and neighbors in providing food, and an informal social atmosphere at the home testifies to the need for a gathering after the funeral.

Whether to have music or not at church ceremonies is a decision best made on the basis of individual preferences, unless the matter is determined by religious authority. Vocal solos, congregational singing, or instrumental music appeal to different groups in different ways. Frequently group custom is strong and innovation resented. Hymns constitute the only acceptable type of songs in certain evangelical and other groups; sentimental songs are prized by some individuals and deprecated by others. Classical instrumental music is preferred above all other types by certain groups. (7). Whether to have one or more speakers at the funeral service, how much group participation should take place at the wake, and what kind, these are all matters to be decided differently in different instances.

The second essential of a satisfying funeral is preparation for it by the family long in advance. On this point there is a maximum of agreement by clergymen, funeral directors, families who have held funerals, and writers on the subject. There is a minimum of observance for reasons which have been noted elsewhere. The only extensively followed form of preparation is insurance for funeral expenses, both in commercial companies and in fraternal orders.

Through pre-arrangements which include comparison of various types of funerals, the family can save itself from the unpleasantness and possible exploitation in the bargaining process. Prearrangements should cover, not only costs and the manner of disposal of the body, but also the family's wishes for the procedure to be followed. Clergymen are often of great help in making preliminary plans. Helpful also are the religious, labor, cooperative and fraternal groups. The advice of a firm or organization which allows for no alternative choices of funeral methods and undertakers is apt to be the least helpful in the end. The less commercial interest the advising group has, the greater the probable value to the inquirer. Whatever advice may be sought from various sources, it is of the utmost importance that the individual's wishes be clearly stated and understood by all members of the family. This helps to avoid confusion and to settle disagreements after the death.

The third essential provision taken in order to make meaningful the series of events at the funeral period is the expeditious disposal of the remains. It need not seem hurried if a plan has been worked out in advance. It should not be so precipitate as to interfere with religious requirements. They can be met, however, in all but a very few instances, within a brief period after death. The purpose of prompt burial, cremation, or other provision is chiefly to give full scope to social and religious aspects, in lesser measure to obviate the prolongation of the agony of separation from the loved body. A third part of the purpose is to minimize the opportunity for morbid curiosity on the part of individuals only slightly affected by the death.

Mechancial devices to make the final disposition of the body brief and to limit handling by anyone, give greatest satisfaction to the family. The image that is conjured up of the operations of embalming and restoration has bothered the recollections of many persons for a period of time following the funeral. For many cremation is by far the most satisfying method. (See Appendix III). Embalming is quite unnecessary, except where some special reason calls for a prolonged period between death and the burial, cremation or other disposition.

The last obligation to the body may be merely a dismissal or necessary leave-taking; or it may be in itself a satisfying act of aiding others and helping to maintain the beneficence of medical science. This is achieved when the corneal tissues are given to bring sight to some unknown but definite person, or the body is relinquished to a medical institution. (See Appendices I and II). Parting with the tangible remains of the deceased must come soon after death. The sooner it happens the fewer memories will be clouded by unnecessary and unpleasant associations and the freer the mind will be to form satisfying recollections of other days. In any case, goodbye is said in no real sense to the lifeless form; it was sensed in the last communication between the living persons, or will be expressed in reminiscences of the coming weeks and years.

The fourth important consideration in an effort to give the funeral period the maximum meaning for all concerned is community or intergroup planning, and multiple observances of the death. Unfortunately the tradition still holds in some quarters, that a wake gathering and a church service satisfy the immediate needs of the family and fulfill the social functions required after a death. Occasionally they do. More often, however, there is a great need to see that each area of companionship, work or other responsibility of the deceased person's life is explored and, if possible, all commemorative observances made known to the family. Mere announcements of the funeral are insufficient. The members of the family usually (and quite properly) refrain from the task.

A funeral society makes a very appropriate agency to search in the various sectors of the life of the deceased person for an understanding of his several interests. A clergyman sometimes undertakes it, but the majority of the clergy does not regard such an undertaking as properly theirs. A close friend, a colleague, or officer of long standing in a civic group seems to be among the most effective agents for the purpose. A member of the family may well suggest the matter to a friend or colleague of the deceased.

The essence of success is prompt action. Many groups fail to note the death of a member merely because it is no specified person's responsibility to observe and initiate action. Very frequently a memorial commensurate with the place the individual has taken in the whole community can be realized only by joint action of several groups. The typical urban community is brought into any action only through its separate groups. The memorial organization for a famous person is an extreme example of what, on a small scale, could magnify the significance of the funeral of the little man and woman.

There may be no joint memorial of any kind effected by the groups, but each in its own way and within its own membership may act as it sees fit. Invariably, however, from any such stimulation a total picture emerges of the statuses and the roles of the deceased person in the community. The friends and relatives who grieve most deeply get from it a sense of recognition that no expensive casket could supply. Frequently, too, planning of this sort induces bringing together at the religious service or other gathering a truer representation of the web of relationships of the deceased than otherwise would be the case. The deep gratification expressed by the family and close friends at the "recognition" of the life that has gone amply compensates for the time and trouble involved.

An observance of the death of a member in each of the major groups to which he belongs gives satisfaction to his associates. It is value of a kind that cannot be gotten from the gathering of all friends and associates; it is a value to the group itself in the nature of improved morale which comes from a recognition of the group's place in the life of the deceased. The sort of commemoration depends on two factors: first the character of the organization, and second the amount of personal interaction usually experienced in it by all the members. The character of the family group, for example, is the determining factor making the gathering of its members an occasion for intimate and often emotional expression of affection and nostalgia, or less often an outbreak of frustration and repressed antagonism.

A group devoted to purely civic or intellectual discussion, particularly if it meets infrequently, seldom holds a memorial meeting but rather records a resolution of appreciation. It is only in the groups which come together often and in which there is face to face interaction that recognition of the death of a member has any great effect on the sense of solidarity or camaraderie. Often the members of a committee or a section of a large organization experience the emotions and satisfactions peculiar to the occasion of the death of a colleague.

Some of the characteristic sentiments of the funeral period emerge at a meeting of an organization devoted to remembrance of a member who has died. Usually differences of attitude and opinion disappear and unity of purpose and emotion emerges. A perspective of time almost invariably becomes apparent, with thoughts turning to the number of years of affiliation of the deceased and to a recapitulation of the stage of development of the group at the time of his joining. There is a spontaneous impulse to inquire into his personal relationships and his other affiliations. Frequently it is the first occasion on which the group sends word to his family. The personal relation of each member of the group to him becomes a poignant consideration.

Not least among emergent thoughts of the members is the consciousness of the purposes and ideals of the group and of the institution of which it is a part.

In the mechanized and routinized subdivisions of labor in modern society the relation of the daily task of one person to the welfare of the whole community is difficult to see or appreciate. The short interlude of final tribute to a colleague offers an unexcelled opportunity for just such appreciation. The line man for a telephone or telegraph company may pursue his task for years more or less unheralded and unsung. However, it is easy to see the peculiar purport of his work in a society which is dependent on intercommunication. For the job boss, the union official, or the officer of an organization to call attention to a like significance of a job, is not only to recognize a fact important in the life of the member, but also to add to the morale of the survivors in the working team.

The most satisfying group observances seem to have three characteristics in common. First, they are held in the place and under the circumstances in which the members usually meet. The physical setting holds many symbols of companionship and common ideals. Second, each of those present has ample opportunity to express his admiration of the departed member. Third, each member who so wishes can find something to do, either individually or in concert with the others.

Mere condolences from a group of co-workers to the family which has suffered bereavement have very slight functional value to the group. Sending them is not to be confused with the observance of the death of a member by the group itself.

The fifth essential of a meaningful funeral is that the whole life that is gone be interpreted in social, ethical and spiritual terms by those deeply moved. The interpretation involves the weaving of the threads of the chief experiences of the deceased, an understanding of his relationships in the community, and an insight into the core of deepest convictions and ideals held by him. One of the most striking qualities of a ceremony in which these three dimensions are portrayed, is the new light that is thrown on the life of the deceased, a light in which he is accorded by those present deeper sympathy than was ever felt for him before. Persons have left such ceremonies yearning for an understanding of themselves by those they love, an understanding that comes with perspective on the total personality in relation to its entire social environment.

The secret of the success experienced by some spokesmen at the funeral ceremony and the relative failure of others, lies not so much in the formula followed as in the artistry required by the occasion. Few possess it and it is not a simple matter to acquire it. It takes time and skill to select the most vital aspects of the dead man's life experiences and to portray them with a combination of objectivity and sympathy. That is why clergymen are loathe merely to go through motions at funerals of persons unknown to them. Several sources usually need to be approached by the funeral organizer for the purpose of preparing himself and helping to bring together an audience that makes the occasion creative. Actually the need for some slight organizing ability, exercised by family, clergyman and leaders in the relevant realms of greatest devotion, is essential. The need is not for long labor but for the aid of insight into the separate spheres in which the life has been lived, not excepting the greatest friendships.

It is not alone the knowledge of the life and values of the deceased that makes the leader's part significant but, since the funeral service is addressed to members of the family and close friends, it is necessary to get a sense of their reactions to the death.

Among the most moving items at funeral services are the brief statements made by close and understanding friends of the deceased. They depict often his own estimate of his life and the basic, perhaps homely, philosophy he held. Suggestions have even been made by a few who thought seriously on the subject that each person, long before he anticipates death, write out his own evaluation of his life's efforts in the light of his ideals, partly that through use of it the leader of the service will be able to make the occasion more convincing.

Artistry of the highest order is required in the leadership of a service to memorialize a life. The basic need is to see that the significant and distinguishing features of the life as a whole are brought out, not as eulogy but as a statement of one person's aspirations for the good life. There is no need for admonitions or "preaching" in the narrow sense. The death itself has done that job; and now spontaneously the individuals in the group experience the yearnings common to those who have lost a close relative or friend.

It takes some skill based on psychological and sociological understanding to recognize the deep yearnings of the participating persons, and to lead their thinking on to the possibilities of endeavor that may answer the yearnings. The ultimate implications must be supplied by the individual listeners themselves; and hence subtlety and suggestion form important features of the artistry of a funerals leadership.

The wake, or lying in state, is an important feature of the public funeral of a distinguished person, but serves a public rather than a family purpose. The chief values of the funeral for the associates of a prominent person are to be gotten from the gathering of a small group, in addition to the public funeral. The functions of the public ceremony for famous individuals are several, but need not concern us here. They are determined by considerations of large social import, and are usually directed by institutional leaders. They are different from the functions of the group or community funeral. For one thing, the more prominent the deceased was the more attention is paid to the body itself.

The sixth essential of a meaningful funeral is a social gathering of the relatives and friends of both the deceased and the surviving members of the family.

A seventh feature that is necessary, if the funeral is to be vitally significant, is the acceleration of the ceremony following the death. It is necessary that it be held while the shock occasioned by the death is still felt. For most persons the period would be a matter of days. There are virtues in holding memorial services later, but virtues of a different nature.

Considerations to be taken into account by the family, the clergy, and others involved in the immediate provisions for the funeral have been outlined. There are provisions to be made also by the community, or groups and institutions in it. Most of them are extensions or improvements on projects proposed or those actually in an experimental stage. The one which most quickly comes to mind is the development and expansion of low cost means of burial, cremation, or other disposal of the body. A particular need of first importance is the building and maintenance of crematoria, preferably by municipalities, so that one is within practical distance of every considerable center of population. With the competition afforded by these several enterprises the private profit funeral directors can be relied upon to offer reasonable prices and wider choices.

A second great need, almost as necessary as the first, is for many more church funeral societies to be formed on broad community bases involving joint efforts of several church and other groups. An excellent beginning is to be found in the Peninsula Funeral Society in Palo Alto, California.

Counseling on a non professional level is given by church funeral societies, and should be increased manyfold. Especially for individuals and families with deep emotional problems there is great need of counseling on a professional level. Two students of family problems have called attention to this fact: "In contrast to the well-defined routines of the funeral is the lack of definition for readjustment afterward. The professional undertaker retires from the scene, and no other professional person enters to aid the members of the family in the next phase of their readjustment. Each family is left more or less to shift for itself, with occasional help and advice from well-meaning relatives and friends." (8, p. 238).

Help in this direction undoubtedly will come as a part of provision for broader purposes, but the dramatic spectacle of bereaved families in need of temporary therapy may aid in persuading agencies to provide it and the public to support it. It is important that those who deal with bereaved families learn from professional sources how to discriminate between the ones who need professional help and the ones who do not. It is as important, too, that the clergy and the funeral directors learn how to refer the cases needing help to the proper agencies.

Another service that welfare agencies can best provide is a central information service in every town or county, preferably as part of the council of social agencies. This service would be competent to state the pertinent facts about private-profit, cooperative, fraternal, church, labor or other paid or volunteer funeral services and to furnish directions for reaching them.

These are all resources provided in the community of direct help in to bereaved families in the actual planning and conduct of funerals. Of even greater importance are the more general and indirect measures society is taking to render life more meaningful and more satisfying to human needs and aspirations. In the long run death will be faced sensibly and courageously more because of the social efforts to enhance the good life than because of any measures to be taken or heroism to be evoked at the time of crisis.

Among the most notable of the measures influencing the mental, social and philosophical development of a growing number of persons are the following. First and foremost is education designed to encourage independent thinking, cooperative habits, faith in human values and a fearless, experimental attitude toward the solution of personal and social problems. It should be noted in this connection that this educational approach has already yielded substantial findings for the guidance of teachers and parents in dealing with children in matters concerning death. (9, pp. 169, 170), (10), (11). (See Appendix IV) Parent education should be included as one of the most promising areas of the whole field of education to develop realistic attitudes toward life and death.

Of only less importance than education is the whole social welfare movement, especially family case wark, and to a lesser extent group work. Individual and group therapy is the most immediate and effective remedy for the worst failures of current funeral practices, and its great extension is one of the ways of overcoming eventually the inadequacies of the culture to serve human needs.

Social settlements and community centers in urban areas, though

pitifully insufficient in numbers, give training and experience in group
association to that part of the city population they reach.   The movements toward decentralization in many fields, neighborhood organization, and some housing developments are operating to give a sense of
community to a considerable number of persons.

Last to be mentioned are the writings which are analyzing the inadequacies of American culture and social organization to meet the
psychic needs of men and women.   Among the authors of them are
Harry A. Overstreet, (12), Erich Fromm, (6), (13), Rollo May, (14).

Conclusion.   It is time for fundamental changes in the conduct of
funerals in the United States.   The evils connected with them have
continued not only for decades but for generations.   Thousands of
families have suffered deprivation because of the unnecessary, unpro-
ductive and unwise expenditures they have made in a pitiful effort to
gain an illusory status for their dead and themselves.   In varying degrees they have also suffered deprivation of the satisfying social and
ethical consolation and inspiration that might have come from mod-
ernly conceived aid in time of grief and mental distress.

The public, or that part of it that can be alerted to social problems,
is well aware of the nature of the problem.   Popular magazine articles
have appeared by the dozen; the most widely read and respected authors from Mark Twain to Erich Fromm have vividly portrayed the
problem in its most dramatic aspects.   Meanwhile it becomes more
difficult to solve, and vested interests bulwark their power and advantages behind the scenes, more assured by the failure of all criticism
to affect their practices that modification actually never will be necessary.   And a defeatist attitude becomes normal for those who see the
evils and would like to witness some reform.

The time has come, not for radical, impetuous and sudden action,
but for a systematic stock taking and an exploration of the nature of
the problem in all its ramifications.   In the extensive, and in many
ways excellent, study a quarter of a century ago by Gebhart, a nar-
now approach was made.   Nothing happened.   It is broad perspective that is needed now, covering all the phases of a social phenomenon
that touches the religious and the social, as well as the economic life
of the community.   It is easy to blame the funeral directors for exploitation in the sale of funeral goods and services.   But the practices
of the funeral directors are symptomatic of deep lying causes; they
do not represent the basic trouble.

It is easy to compile some economic facts and then to look for a cure in the form of a specific economic remedy. Social evils are not cured that way, however. For an approach to the problem of the funeral it is now necessary to look at it both in a comprehensive light as a total complex of causal factors and effects, and in its many sided, social, cultural, economic, even political aspects. It is a concern of everyone. Perhaps that is why so little has been done about it: it is not the particular business of anyone or any group. When something is done about it, and sooner or later something substantial must be done, the group that tackles the problem should include top level and responsible representatives of many community areas of endeavor. The reason for such representation is that the funeral has to do with the values which the community serves, the ideals of all people everywhere.

This is not a partisan matter. The basic interests of all groups are identical in the final analysis. The practices and dogmas of every faith cannot only be fully respected and protected, but the influence of each can be extended and strengthened. Certainly, free enterprise is in not the slightest danger, despite the fact that it constitutes the red herring that has been pulled across the trail in certain local disagreements. It is not to the advantage of free enterprise that its name be invoked in defense of practices inconsistent with its own principles. It is distinctly to its advantage to have the full light of impartial search thrown on any sector of business and ultimately to see perfected whatever adjustments are necessary to bring about fair play in all business relations.

Reform in the funeral industry is not even a good reason for conflict among proponents of public, private profit and private cooperative enterprise. As is the case in the field of housing, there is an area appropriate to each. Every person should have assurance that a "decent funeral" will be given his remains. If his resources are not sufficient for that purpose, it is the responsibility of the public to furnish minimal provision in the manner in which it provides old age security. It should come, not as charity from any group, nor as the surplus from an overcharge on funerals of more wealthy customers. Private provision is made by some of the families who have the means to insure for themselves the modest funerals they can afford. They constitute a group who will not need to take advantage of public provision, and will never be content to patronize a funeral business except as it is organized and directed by themselves without profit to outsiders.

It is in the interest of the funeral directors themselves to have the business put on a business basis. Their tribulations are due primarily to the fact that it is not operating according to the laws of the market. Thoroughgoing reorganization of the business to meet the needs of the nation on an efficient, economic basis would do wonders for the funeral directors as well as for their customers. Furthermore, an improvement in the basic cultural values espoused by undertakers would lift them in public esteem high above their present level.

Hopefully there will be many approaches to the problem from several angles. There are a few to be found at present, though none is comprehensive enough to cover the facets of the problem. None is comprehensive enough in terms of affiliations and interests of its supporters. None is operating with adequate funds to amass the facts that are necessary for any dependable conclusions.

One way to approach the problem is through an independent commission created to make studies of the main aspects of the problem, to conduct open discussions in which consuming, commercial, religious, cultural and social representatives participate, and eventually to act as an information and advisory agency. The commission might best be composed of a majority representing community interests: clergy, educators, social workers, officials of funeral societies of fraternal, church or other affiliation, and the medical schools and research institutions. In addition, the clients of the funeral establishments, businessmen and the funeral directors themselves should be represented.

Through such a commission, or other unbiased agency, it is essential that research be conducted into several fields: the conditions imposed on the customer's choice of the style and cost of the funeral he desires; the workings of social security, public assistance benefit provisions in the light of funeral benefits from all other sources, including labor-management contracts; the legislation of the various states regulating licensing of funeral directors and the composition as well as operations of state boards; the laws of the several states regarding sanitary provisions, and particularly laws compelling procedures costly to the customers which have little or no relation to the public welfare; the lobbying activities of funeral associations; the mortuary schools and the feasibility of affiliation of them with colleges, with a view to supplementing the technical training with more education of sociological, philosophical and cultural nature; the operation of public provision of funeral service abroad; the means of furnishing the personal counseling needed by individuals deeply disturbed by death in the family; the economics of cemetery corporations and casket companies and their relations to funeral establishments, as well as the connection between the latter and florists.

Research personnel appropriate for the purpose in hand should include not only economic competence but anthropological, sociological, psychological and even political science competence as well. From an objective point of view the defects in funeral practice consist partly in failure to utilize relevant scientific methods to serve the cultural purpose in hand.

A commission for inquiry, research and discussion on a high level would soon be qualified to furnish an information and advisory service to groups and agencies throughout the country, and to have published monographs as well as articles in periodicals. Working locally in connection with it, or in lieu of it, coordinated activity in communities is needed to furnish information and advice to individuals and agencies, and to stimulate mutual cooperative activity of churches, civic groups, fraternal societies and labor organizations.

It requires an exercise of faith to expect that the present neglect of the problem by the public will soon be transformed into mutual planning and activity. However, projects demanding more effort, and productive of less potential benefit, have come into existence through competent, high minded leadership. An interested, warm and generous response from the people of the United States to projects of an altruistic nature is just as characteristic as their neglect of other matters.

More potent still is the realization, unformulated and unexpressed though it may be, that in the presence of the death of a loved one human natures rises to its most sublime heights. Any effort to lessen the anguish of bereavement and to foster the fullest opportunities to experience social and spiritual uplift at that time of crisis, is certain to elicit enthusiastic response from institutions and organizations as well as from the great majority of individuals in the country.

INSTRUCTIONS FOR THE DONATION OF EYES TO
THE EYE-BANK FOR SIGHT RESTORATION

The most satisfactory way to learn about donation of the eyes is to write directly to The Eye-Bank for Sight Restoration, Inc., 210 East 64th Street, New York 21, New York, (telephone Templeton 8-9200) and from it receive the *Form for Persons Wishing to Donate Their Eyes After Death* and the booklet, *A Gift Like the Gifts of God,* which explains the functions of the Eye-Bank and the procedure for anyone to follow who wishes to donate his eyes. As explained in the booklet, from which the following statements are quoted or the substance of them taken, the Eye-Bank's need for eyes to be donated at time of death is very urgent because there are over 20,000 known cases today who could have their sight restored through a corneal transplant, and the demand is increasing. To serve the need is a privilege given to this generation by the scientists, who in 1944 learned after long experimentation how to restore sight to those who have lost it through corneal defect caused by disease or accident. Since that date the soundness of the techniques used has been proved by the success achieved in its use in over 90 per cent of the favorable cases.

Regardless of the part of the country in which a person may live, either or both eyes can be donated to help restore the sight of someone now blind from corneal defect. Since the statement of Pope Pius XII on May 14, 1956, Catholics as well as others are at full liberty to agree to corneal transplantations. There are no fees of any kind for the removal of the eyes. Since the recipient pays nothing for the eyes to be used for the corneal grafting operation, the donor neither makes nor receives any payment. There is no disfigurement.

The question of age has no bearing on donating the eyes; if the tissue is healthy, the eyes of a stillborn baby or an old person can be used. The fact that a person has worn glasses or has suffered previous eye injury has no bearing on the usefulness of corneal tissue. Furthermore the cause of death has little significance with regard to usefulness of corneal tissue. The decision to donate eyes should therefore be made without question of possible defect in them, leaving that consideration to the experts at the Eye-Bank, and knowing that, except in extremely rare instances, the donation will be a great blessing. Surgeons who have registered cases with the Eye-Bank, each of whom when the time comes sees that an operating room and hospital bed is available and the patient ready, are notified in turn when eyes become available. For the purpose only doctors contact the Eye-Bank, and it is therefore impossible for a donor to designate any specific individual for his benefaction.

It gives additional gratification to any one contemplating the gift of his eyes to know that they are returned to the Eye-Bank and used for pathological study after the corneal tissue is removed. Through the study a body of information for ophthalmologists is being built up that redounds to the benefit of other sufferers. A corneal clinic is maintained by the Eye-Bank at which patients with corneal defects can secure diagnoses and consultation.

In order that the donation may benefit some afflicted person it is essential that certain arrangements be made before death, and that instructions be left for wife, husband or next of kin to follow afterward.

(1) When it has been decided to donate eyes, the prospective donor should communicate with the Eye-Bank to secure the form to be filled out (quoted below), and the pamphlet spoken of above, if they have not already been acquired.

(2) The form provided by the Eye-Bank should be filled out. It reads in part: "I herewith express the wish to donate, at time of death, to the Eye-Bank for Sight Restoration, Inc., or to an affiliated bank, both or either of my eyes for such use as said Eye-Bank may see fit with regard to all or any part of my eyes."

Date, signature, address of donor, and signature of the witness are to be given. The witness can be a member of the family.

(3) When the form has been filled out, signed, and witnessed, it should be given to the next-of-kin, who will notify the hospital authorities or attending physician at time of death, and they, in turn, will notify the Eye-Bank any time of the day or night.

(4) If death occurs in a home within driving distance of New York City the spouse or next of kin should notify the Eye-Bank immediately in order that it may have the doctor come promptly to remove the eyes. In other sections arrangements must be made with a hospital. In any case speed is essential.

(5) If the donor is in a hospital, any hospital, and there is a possi-

bility of death, the hospital authorities should be informed that the eyes are to be donated to the Eye-Bank.

The donor does not have to make any arrangements with the hospital for removal of the eyes. After death, the eyes are removed by qualified personnel in the hospital and sent to the Eye-Bank.

The affiliated eye-banks are:

Boston Eye-Bank, 243 Charles St., Boston 14, Mass., Telephone: Lafayette 3-8230.

Illinois Eye-Bank, c/o Illinois Society for the Prevention of Blindness, 203 N. Wabash Ave., Chcago 1, Ill., Telephone: Central 6-8479.

The Eye-Bank for Restoring Sight, Inc., 1608 W. Academy St., Winston-Salem, N. C., Telephone: Doctors Exchange 2-5022.

California has its own eye-banks, unaffiliated with the national group:

University of California Eye-Bank, University of California Medical Center, San Francisco 22, Cal.

The Stanford Eye-Bank, 2398 Sacramento St., San Francisco 15, California.

DIRECTIONS FOR GIFT OF THE BODY
TO A MEDICAL SCHOOL

1. When the decision is made to give the body, a nearby medical school which is authorized by law to confer the degree of doctor of medicine should be communicated with to see if it accepts bodies.

2. The donor should make an affidavit, which is witnessed, stating it is his wish that his body be turned over to the medical school after his death, and instructing his wife (or husband), or if he has no spouse or she should predecease him, then his next of kin, to have the body given to the school named.

3. The husband, wife or next of kin, should make affidavit, also witnessed, stating that he acquiesces in the wish of the donor, and making request of the specific medical school to accept the body and devote it to medical, anatomical or surgical science and study. The two statements may both be included in one affidavit and signed by the donor and his spouse, or by him and his next of kin. The affidavit, or affidavits, is kept by the spouse or next of kin, to be given to the representative of the medical school after death has occurred.

It should be understood that the costs of transportation of the body, if requested, will be borne by the family of the donor or the estate. They are nominal, or often for short distances, nil.

It is not necessary, ordinarily, to inform the medical school beforehand that the body will be given to it eventually.

4. After the death has occurred, the spouse or next of kin should make sure that a certificate of death is in his hands, signed by the attending physician. In case there has been no physician in attendance at the time of death, a certificate of death can be secured from the local health officer in the health department, or where it exists, from the office of the chief medical examiner, also in the health department. The certificate should be secured immediately.

5. The medical school should be informed promptly after the death. The affidavit or affidavits mentioned above, together with the certificate of death, should be gotten to the person from the medical school

in charge of transportation of the body in order that he may secure a permit for transportation from the office of the health department which issues permits. It may be possible to meet the agent of the medical school at the office granting burial permits.

6. Having secured the permit for transportation of the body, the medical school agent will remove it to the school.

It is possible, but wholly unnecessary, to have an undertaker secure the certificate of death and the transit permit.

The body may be picked up from any place, including: home, hospital, or funeral parlor. Occasionally it is necessary to insist on the disposition of the body as the donor and the spouse or next of kin have previously determined. The spouse or next of kin has full legal authority and responsibility.

Embalming should be left to the medical school.

If the eyes have been bequeathed to the Eye-Bank, they should be taken, by prearrangement, before the body is removed to the medical school.

In case the death has occurred from a communicable disease the body must be disposed of by a licensed undertaker.

CREMATION IN THE UNITED STATES

Cremation is the reduction of the body to its basic elements by heat. In an hour and a half a process is completed that takes nature twenty to thirty years. It is largely a process of evaporation, since the great bulk of the body is water. The remains consist of six to twelve pounds of white ashes or bone fragments. Various types of chambers are used, all on the principle of a gas retort, utilizing gas or oil to produce temperatures of 1800 to 2500 degrees Fahrenheit. It is a clean, thorough method of body disposal, devoid of offensive features. The dust remains are placed in an urn, kept in a niche in a columbarium, or in the spot decided upon by the family of the deceased person, or scattered in a fashion determined by sentiment.

In its primitive form cremation is of ancient origin; in its modern, more complete fashion it is less than a century old in the United States. The first crematorium in this country was erected in 1876 in Washington, Pennsylvania, although articles about it had appeared as early as 1737. The New York Cremation society was organized in 1881 and the national organization, The Cremation Association of America, in 1913. The original impulse, following the European pattern, sprang from a belief that burial created an unsanitary environment in the neighborhood of cemeteries, coupled with concern for the space that burial grounds were pre-empting from use by the community.

The initial leadership, largely of physicians and sanitarians, gave way in time to that of a commercial nature by the proprietors of crematories. Less has been written on the subject since the late eighteen eighties, although an occasional article can be found in current periodicals. The growth has been considerable, however, at varying rates. The Cremation Association of America prints figures indicating increase of cremation for the last twenty years to a total of 299,202 for the 1949-53 interval. It reports also declining five year rates of increase, from 1934 of 24 per cent, 24 per cent, 16 1/2 per cent, 12 per cent. Other sources give something like 72,000 as the number of cremations taking place annually. It is safe to conclude that cremations account for 5 per cent, or less, of funerals each year. Cremation, however, is firmly established and will continue indefinitely to be used, probably by increasing numbers of families. The movement in Europe, where pressure of limited space is greater than here, is growing more rapidly.

The process has been adopted most enthusiastically in the Pacific Coast states, where in 1949-53 approximately half of all cremations in the country occurred, and where one in six funerals include cremation. On the other hand, in the more populous Middle Atlantic states, New York, Pennsylvania and New Jersey, and in other sections of the country in which tradition is relatively strong, the proportion of cremations to all funerals is small. There are more than two hundred crematories in the United States, ten of them government operated: six by states, two by counties, one by a municipality, and one by the Federal Government in Washington, D. C.

The case in favor of cremation includes the two points mentioned, of sanitary benefits and economy of space, as well as consolation of sorrowing friends and relatives in the method, avoiding the horrors of slow decay, and allowing for the satisfaction of a permanent memorial in the inurnment, if that is desired. Lastly it is maintained cremation provides the possibility of disposal of the body at much less cost. Advanced less often are two considerations: one, that cremation is actually more reverent than burial since the body need not be handled or disturbed after death, and two, that shipping of ashes in a container is infinitely easier, safer from a sanitary point of view, and inexpensive as compared to shipping embalmed remains.

Rejection of the cremation method rests on several bases. Probably tradition is the largest factor operating against its use. Sentiment associated with burial is another. Opposition from the Roman Catholic Church and the Orthodox Jewish group constitutes a potent force preventing cremation on a large scale. The core of objection from these two sources lies in the belief that cremation hinders or prevents resurrection of the body, and that it is not sufficiently respectful of the body which has been the temple of the soul.

The process is resisted, too, on the ground that it destroys evidence of crime by preventing autopsies. From the same standpoint it makes identification impossible, and thereby renders decisions on insurance and settlement of estates impossible if they depend upon identification after death and disposal of the body. To meet this objection in part the Pacific Coast states and certain others require that cremated remains be placed permanently in dedicated interment property to aid in keeping state records. It is difficult to believe that the relatively small value of the remains as a record is the only motivating factor on the part of the persons and groups which secured the passage of the legislation in question. A very few states prohibit scattering of the ashes. One argument against it, occasionally advanced, is the questionable statement that the ashes are composed of minute bone particles and do not unite favorably with the soil. Whether by burial or cremation the ultimate residue of the dissolution process is the mineral constituents of the body. The aesthetic argument, used in opposition to scattering the ashes, is only a counterpart of the aesthetic repulsion to the process and effects of body decay.

REACTIONS OF CHILDREN TO DEATH AND FUNERALS

Aggravating the burden and grief at the time of death in the family is the perplexity as to methods of dealing with children. Their responses to the loss are different, at least in mode of expression, from those of adults, and therefore frequently misunderstood. Students of child development have made available in printed form the information needed to deal sympathetically and intelligently with children, the elements of which should be understood by all parents of growing children. Pamphlets are available at very small cost to be obtained by writing for them. Of especial value are: *When Children Ask About Death,* by Florence W. Klaber, available from the Society for Ethical Culture, 2 West 64th St., New York 23, N.Y.; *Helping Children Accept Death,* by Margaret S. Mahler, M.D., and *Helping Your Child to Understand Death,* by Anna W. M. Wolf, to be secured from The Child Study Association of America, 132 East 74th St., New York 21, New York, and *When You Lose a Loved One,* by Ernest Osborne, published by Public Affairs Pamphlets, 22 East 38th St., New York 16, N.Y. Another source is *The Encyclopedia of Child Care and Guidance,* Sidonie Matsner Gruenberg, Editor, Doubleday & Company, Garden City, N. Y. In that volume the articles on *Death, Explaining to Children* and on *Death in the Family* are most helpful. Others of value are on *Anxiety* and *How to Handle Children's Fears.*

Among the main points made by the experts is the need for all children to become acquainted early with the cycle of life as they watch animals in the home or the school, and in so doing to learn how death is part of all living. Playing funeral at the death of a pet may be a protection against violent reactions to a later death in the family. When children ask about death they are to be answered without evasion but on the level each of his understanding, and not at greater length than his attention and interest warrant. There is need, too, as in all other aspects of child care, to know the child's fantasies, from observation of play activities, listening to his stories and talk and in other ways. More than one author inveighs against the common fallacy of explaining death as sleep and thereby laying the child open to possible disappointment at a critical time. How the parent expresses himself is of as great importance as what he says.

A deep religious faith serves to give parent and child assurance. It will furnish the answers for those who have it to the questions children sometimes raise about the place to which the dead go. For parents who do not have the answer an honest reply, such as "we don't know," is better than false or equivocal statements. In every way preparation for death is superior to the shielding of children from knowledge of it, or experience with it, as it occurs in the child's environment.

The same generalization applies at the time when death comes to one of the family; neither its occurrence nor the grief of the parents are to be hidden from the child. Exclusion from their presence or from some knowledge of their grief is perhaps the hardest for him to bear. His anxiety is lessened if he knows what is happening around him. He may not know how to handle his own grief and either dramatize it in an effort to behave in the manner he thinks is expected of him, or act as if he does not care if he thinks he has been excluded from the family mourning. It requires parental understanding to help him know what his feelings are, and to express them without pretense or restraint.

Deprivation of the company of brother, mother, grandparent, or other person may cause the child to feel that his world is insecure. If one goes both parents may, or he himself may die. He may also feel that he is now different from other children since he has no father, or brother, or grandparent. The weight of insecurity may arouse anger and resentment that he has been deserted. Almost invariably a sense of guilt oppresses him. In impulsive reaction to a denial of privilege or other act that has displeased him, the child may have previously expressed dislike for the person who now lies dead. He may even, in childish petulance, have expressed the wish that the other die. It had been only a momentary wish, but then, when death occurs, it may seem to him to have been brought about by his hasty words. He needs sympathetic support and help in arriving at an appreciation of his own spontaneous actions and the understanding that adults have of his behavior. Under great stress at the family crisis, neurotic symptoms may possibly appear, requiring professional treatment. Should the child look at the corpse? The professional advice is: not at too early an age. If, however, he is curious it is best to satisfy his desires. As with adults the memory of the living person is the most satisfying.

One author has summarized the emotional responses a child may exhibit when death comes to someone dear to him: sorrow because of the separation, to be met with the truth, tempered to his understanding; anger that life has done this thing to him, in answer to which he needs to learn to accept misfortune; anxiety and a possible swift turning to others that a surviving parent finds difficult to understand and accept; guilt that requires patient discussion; and grief that he must be helped to meet in his way, often a way different from that of the adult. Extra show of affection, stories that give child-world cues to understanding, mutual talk—these may uncover worries that persist. In patient, sympathetic, perhaps often repeated experiences of parental listening, as well as expressions of assurance, the child regains a sense of security.

Added responsibility may rest on the surviving parent after the death, and it may be the basis in part for placing more responsibility on the child. Care must be taken that it is not beyond his comprehension and normal inclinations, nor in such amount that he is deprived of full opportunity for play and typical childish activities. He should not have a sense of unusual responsibility resting on his shoulders. Reference to the parent who has gone is not tabu; rather it is helpful to the child to keep the memory green in the unforced ways that offer themselves in the course of family living. Adjustments to developments in the changed situation come more acceptably in that way.

It is of the utmost importance that the surviving parent or other members of the family help the child at his level, and in his way to feel assurance that the world is a secure one in which to live, that life is worth the living in the finest possible way.

PRINCIPAL ANTHROPOLOGICAL THEORIES

Emile Durkheim. For Durkheim the funeral is to be explained as a sacred rite. In 1912 his *Elementary Forms of Religious Life* (1) appeared, in which he developed his theory of religion from observation and analysis of primitive cultures. He believed that to study the subject most satisfactorily one should go back to its simple forms found in primitive social groups; there he found that religious "representations" express the collective realities, the common value attitudes. Ideas and attitudes belong in one or the other of the categories sacred and profane, and religion is the unified system of beliefs and practices relative to sacred things.

Rites, of which the funeral is one, constitute a manner of acting in the midst of the assembled group to maintain or re-create certain mental states, especially through the manipulations of symbols, in order to strengthen the collective sentiments and bring the members together. Religious rites and collective re-creations are so close that men pass from one to the other without a break. After a religious rite men enter profane life with increased zest and courage. The family which had felt lessened and had experienced a lack of moral unity, assembles, feels a renewal of its unity and proves its solidarity to the other members of the group. During the ceremony sadness and anger grip the relatives and they engage in a variety of violent acts to answer their need of avenging death.

Bronislaw Malinowski. Twenty two years later Malinowski, in *Magic, Science and Religion and Other Essays* (2), developed a theory somewhat at variance with that of Durkheim. Regarding the separation of the secular and the religious expressions of the group, he maintains that "in primitive societies religion arises to a great extent from purely individual sources. Secondly, society as a crowd is by no means always given to the production of religious beliefs or even to religious states of mind, while collective effervescence is often of an entirely secular nature. Thirdly, tradition, the sum total of certain rules and cultural achievements, embraces, and in primitive societies keeps in a tight grip, both Profane and Sacred." (2, p. 31).

Under primitive conditions, according to Malinowski, death is of the greatest importance as a source of religion, while death and immortality are the poignant theme of man's forebodings. Death breaks the normal course of life and shakes the moral foundations of society; it threatens the very cohesion and solidarity of the group. Two impulses contend in the minds of the survivors: love of the dead and a loathing of the corpse, an impulse to preserve the body and a conflicting one to annihilate it. This generalization is also to be found in other anthropological studies.

E. D. Chapple, C. S. Coon and A. L. Van Gennep. The work of Chapple and Coon (3) comes closest to an adequate analysis of the modern funeral, from my point of view, of any of the scientific writings. Their intent was to use a method that would give a rigidly scientific control to their operations, an attempt to explain the phenomena of human relations in terms of measurements on a time scale. Subjective interpretations were ignored and maximum attention placed on a quantitative scheme of observation and exposition. It consisted in the first place, of counting the "originations," or approaches (verbal or not) of one of two persons to the other, and responses of the second. Particularly the rates of interaction, in the sense of originations and responses, as well as the alternation of silences and actions, became a fundamental concept in the theoretical system they built up. In their work "set events," involving a group of persons reacting simultaneously to a leader's origination or some happening which affects them all, are distinguished from pair interactions. Out of the patterns of pair and set interactions a dynamic structure becomes manifest.

Through the process of conditioning, an equilibrium, a recognized order of interaction, becomes established, creating the basis of social stability. In the event of a crisis the equilibrium is broken and the customary pattern of interaction of each individual within the "set" is disturbed. The means of surmounting the crisis and establishing a new equilibrium with something like the original rates of interaction, is furnished by the shaman, or other religious guide, who assumes the place of leader until the new order is under way.

The two authors, writing in 1942, built on the foundations laid by Arnold Van Gennep (4) in 1909, to explain how "the change in the interaction rates, upsetting the equilibria of the individuals concerned, is countered by a series of techniques requiring the interactions of the disturbed individuals in specific and habitual ways. These techniques are called *rituals,* and if the rituals are associated with the crises derived from the actions of a single individual, they are called *Rites of Passage,* a term applied by Van Gennep." (3, p. 398). Chapple and Coon proceed to show how the three stages occurring in the reestablishment of the new equilibrium, namely separation from the other members of the former group; the transition period (Van Gennep's "marge") and incorporation (l'agrégation) into the new group or arrangement of the old, show changed rates of interaction. In separation there is a reduced rate, in transition an increased rate within the new system, and in incorporation a rate resembling that of the period preceding the crisis.

Rites of passage, among which the funeral is prominent, made necessary by acts of individuals creating crises for the whole group, are contrasted with rites of intensification which are the rituals called for by misfortunes affecting directly all members of the group, and hence requiring reorganization of interaction in every institution. The techniques of reestablishing equilibrium, i.e., rituals, consist in acting out in dramatic fashion the pattern of relationships required in the new situation, in which the individual begins again.

The complexity of the ceremonies and the extent of the relationships affected depend upon the ramifications of the relationships of the individual whose acts have caused the disturbance. An infant's death or that of an old man cause little disturbance, since neither has recently interacted widely with other persons, and hence is followed by a simple ceremony or by none. An adult male's death, on the other hand, would be the occasion for a thorough going funeral, while that of a king or chieftain would be observed with extraordinary features. Further, the elaborateness of the ceremonies varies according to the relation of the group to the other institutions in the society, and according to the quantitative value of changes which have resulted from the particular crisis that has occurred. Symbols play a large part in rituals, depicting the repeated activities and relationships, although they are of less relative importance in rites of passage, including the funeral. Spatial relations between celebrants at rituals takes on symbolic meaning.

As has been said in the Preface, I found the strictly behavioristic approach of great value in the formulation of a concept of the basic structure and scope of the funeral. To that extent, at least, I have in this present study followed in the footsteps of Chapple and Coon. Beyond that point, however, I have used other methods as they seemed best fitted to the purposes in hand.

Throughout the present study the criterion of degree of interaction

between members of the respective groups has been uppermost, as is
true in the practice of many social scientists as well as Chapple and
Coon. The latter ascribe more relative importance to the leader-
follower relation than I, and less to spontaneous acts of individuals.
This difference in findings may be due to the difference in methods,
particularly since, because of the procedure followed by the two authors, origination by the leader in any set event is a first hypothesis.

A further difference may or may not relate to methods employed,
namely, the much greater emphasis placed by Chapple and Coon on
the conditioning process as the potent influence in rituals to bring
about equilibria in reaction rates between celebrants. No one, be-
haviorist or not, can doubt its efficacy, it would seem to me. Nevertheless, when an effort is made, despite all its difficulties and possible
pitfalls, to learn what the subjective accompaniment of overt acts is,
the depth and power of convictions and feelings are striking. At least
it is so in the case of funerals. It seems therefore of greatest service,
in an exposition of the phenomenon that has been scrutinized, to describe it in the terms that carry the fullest weight of meaning.

In other ways it appears to me the theoretical framework of Chapple
and Coon is applicable in greater measure to simpler than to the
complex, urban world, so far as the funeral ritual is concerned. The
three stages of separation, transition and incorporation are observable
but in increasingly weaker manifestations as one moves from small
groups to larger, and especially to metropolitan conditions. Perhaps
to say that much is merely to deny that rituals apply in large groupings devoid of unified systems of symbols. It is for this reason that
the funeral of the very prominent man, in my estimation, falls in a
different category of ceremony from that of the more modest citizen,
a distinction not in accordance with the findings of the two authors
in question.

These are not minor points, but they do not negate the essential
similarity of the present study and the basically important works of
Gennep and Chapple and Coon. Perhaps the differences, other than
those of method, are to be accounted for largely by the narrow focus
of the study of the modern funeral as compared to the broad sweep
of the generalizations of social and cultural processes. Even more
obvious is the distinction in the audiences addressed, in the one case
scientists and students in the discipline of scientific training, in the
other all persons who have an interest in the funeral.

REFERENCES

II

1. Thomas D. Elliot, ' The Bereaved Family," *Annals of the American Academy of Political and Social Science,* 160. (March, 1932).
2. Paul H. Landis, *Your Marriage and Family Living,* New York and London, McGraw Hill Book Company, 1946.
3. Robert Laton Dickinson and Lura Beam, *A Thousand Marriages: A Medical Study of Sex Adjustment,* Baltimore, Williams and Wilkins, 1931.
4. Willard Waller, *The Family, a Dynamic Interpretation,* New York, Cordon Co., 1938.
5. Thomas D. Eliot, *Family Crises and Ways of Meeting Them,* quoted in Evelyn Duvall and Reuben Hill, *When You Marry,* Boston, Heath, 1945.
6. James Agee, *A Death in the Family,* New York, McDowell, Obolensky, Inc., 1958.

III

1. *Analysis of Attitudes Toward Funeral Directors,* National Funeral Directors' Association, 1948.
2. James Agee, *A Death in the Family,* New York, McDowell, Obolensky, Inc., 1958.

V

1. Charles M. Brown, "Reducing the High Cost of Dying," *Christian Century,* L III, 43 (October 21, 1936).
2. "Functions of the Modern Mortician," *American Funeral Director,* LV, 12 (December, 1932).
3. Paul Blanshard, *The Nation,* C XXVII, 3311 (December 19, 1928).
4. *Analysis of Attitudes Toward Funeral Directors,* Milwaukee, National Funeral Directors Association, 1948.
5. Wilber M. Krieger, "Facts Help Interpret Funeral Service," *Casket and Sunnyside,* L XXXIV, 9 (September 1954).
6. John C. Gebhart, *Funeral Costs: What They Average, Are They Too High? Can They Be Reduced?* New York-London, Putnam, 1928.
7. Wilber M. Krieger, *Successful Funeral Service Management,* New York, Prentice-Hall, Inc., 1951.

VI

1. Edward A. Martin, "Psychology in Action," *Casket and Sunnyside,* 85, 2 (February, 1955).
2. Attorney General Nathan L. Goldstein (New York State), December 28, 1954.

3. Joseph S. Abbundi, "A Funeral Director Protests to New York State's Attorney General," *Casket and Sunnyside,* L XXXV, 2 (February. 1955).

4. Advertisement, Dodge Chemical Company, *Southern Funeral Director,* LXV, 11 (November, 1951).

5. *Analysis of Attitudes Toward Funeral Directors,* National Funeral Directors Association, 1948.

6. Hugh Stevenson Tigner, "A Foray into Funeral Customs," *Christian Century,* LIV, 41 (October 13, 1932).

7. *When Death Comes* (pamphlet), Elgin, Ill., Elgin Ministerial Association, 1948.

8. A. L. Kershaw, "Death, Burial and the Christian Church," *The Pastor,* 18, 2 (October, 1954).

VII

1. A. L. H. Street, Attorney at law and author of *Street's Mortuary Jurisprudence,* "Right to Permit Mortuaries in Twilight Zones," *American Funeral Director,* LXXI, 11 (November, 1948).

2. J. D. Stephens, "A Helping Hand for the Underprivileged," *American Funeral Director,* LVIII, 4 (April, 1935).

3. McDill McCown Gassman, *Daddy Was an Undertaker,* New York, Vantage Press, 1952.

4. News item, *Southern Funeral Director,* LXV, 7 (July, 1951).

5. Charles A. Renouard, "Embalming, the Basis of Professional Rank," quoting Fred A. Taylor, Assistant Director, California Department of Professional and Vocational Standards, *Casket and Sunnyside,* LXXXI, 11 (November, 1951).

6. "Challenge of 1952," editorial, *Casket and Sunnyside,* LXXXII, 1 (January, 1952).

7. Senate Bills No. 253-256, *Forum,* 17, 9 (July, 1952).

8. Everett Cherrington Hughes, "Work and the Self," Chapter 13 in John H. Rohrer and Muzafer Sherif, *Social Psychology at the Crossroads,* New York, Harper and Brothers, 1951.

9. "Safeguarding Our Professional Status, Professionalism Must Be Backed by a Sound Business Structure," *American Funeral Director,* LVII, 12 (December, 1934).

10. "Funeral Service People Grow in Stature," editorial, *Southern Funeral Director,* LXV, 11 (November, 1951).

11. *Analysis of Attitudes Toward Funeral Directors,* Milwaukee, National Funeral Directors Association, 1948.

12. A. M. Carr-Saunders and P. A. Wilson, *The Professions,* Oxford, Clarendon Press, 1933.

13. A. M. Carr-Saunders and P. A. Wilson, "Professions," in *Encyclopedia of the Social Sciences,* 12.

14. Talcott Parsons, *Essays in Sociological Theory, Pure and Applied,* Glencoe, Ill., The Free Press, 1949.

VIII

1. Ralph E. Houseman, "What I Know About You," Proceedings: 68th Annual Convention, National Funeral Directors Association, *The Director*, XX, 2 (February, 1950).

2. *Funeral Service as a Vocation* (pamphlet), Milwaukee, National Funeral Directors' Association, 1945.

3. Interview with Wilber M. Krieger, September 13, 1950.

4. *Vital Statistics of the United States*, 1952, Vol. I., U. S. Department of Health, Education and Welfare, Public Health Service, National Office of Vital Statistics.

5. *U. S. Census of Business*, 1948, Volume VI Service Trades, Census Bureau, U. S. Department of Commerce, Washington, 1952.

6. Wilber M. Krieger, "Facts Help Interpret Funeral Service," *Casket and Sunnyside*, LXXXIV, 9, (September, 1954).

7. Census of Manufacturers, 1947, Vol. 11, U. S. Department of Commerce, Bureau of the Census, Washington, D. C.: U. S. Government Printing Offiice, 1949, "Morticians' Goods."

8. Albert R. Kates, A Reply to the Federal Council of Churches, *American Funeral Director*, LXVII, 2 (December, 1944).

9. "New York Applies Ounce of Prevention Technique to Field of Public Relations," *American Funeral Director*, LXXI, 4 (April, 1948).

10. "Editorial Outbursts," *Southern Funeral Director*, LXV, 12 (December, 1951).

X

1. Clarence Schettler, "Relation of City-Size to Economic Services," *American Sociological Review*, 8, 1 (February, 1943).

2. Robert W. Habenstein and William M. Lamers, *The History of American Funeral Directing*, Milwaukee, Bulfin Printers, 1955.

3. Joseph H. Douglass, "The Funeral of 'Sister President'," in T. M. Newcomb and E. L. Hartley, *Readings in Social Psychology*, New York, Henry Holt and Company, 1947.

XI

1. Graham Taylor, *Pioneering on Social Frontiers*, Chicago, University of Chicago Press, 1930.

2. Mark Twain, *Life on the Mississippi*, New York and London, Harper Brothers, 1901.

3. Quincy L. Dowd, *Funeral Management and Costs: a World Survey of Burial and Cremation*, Chicago, University of Chicago Press, 1921.

4. James Myers, Jr., *Cooperative Funeral Associations*, Cooperative League of the U. S. A., 1946.

5. Jerry Voorhis, *The Cooperatives Look Ahead*, Public Affairs Pamphlet, No. 32, Public Affairs Committee, 1952.

6. The Undertaker Collects the Insurance, *U.A.W.-C.I.O. Ammunition,* VIII, 11 (November, 1950).

7. Coop Cradle to Coop Grave, *U.A.W.-C.I.O. Ammunition,* IX, 7 (July, 1951).

8. *A Gift Like the Gifts of God,* The Eye-Bank for Sight Restoration, Inc., 238 East 64th St., New York 21, N. Y.

XII

1. Thomas Wolfe, *Look Homeward Angel,* New York, C. Scribner's Sons, 1947.

2. Sam Astrachan, *An End to Dying,* New York, Farrar, Straus and Cudahy, 1956.

3. John Dewey, *A Common Faith,* New Haven, Yale University Press, 1934.

4. Victor E. Frankl, M.D., *The Doctor and the Soul: An Introduction to Logotherapy,* New York, Alfred A. Knopf, 1955.

5. Robert Raible, "Death Be Not Proud," *Christian Register,* 130, 7, (August, 1951).

6. Erich Fromm, *Escape from Freedom,* New York, Rinehart, 1941.

7. Corliss Lamont, *A Humanist Funeral Service,* Boston, The Beacon Press, 1947.

8. Evelyn Mills Duvall and Reuben Hill, *When You Marry,* Boston, D. C. Heath, 1945.

9. Sidonie Matsner Gruenberg, editor, *The Encyclopedia of Child Care and Guidance,* Doubleday and Co., Garden City, N. Y., 1954.

10. Margaret S. Mahler, M. D., *Helping Children to Accept Death* (pamphlet), New York Child Study Association of America, 1950.

11. Florence W. Klaber, *When Children Ask About Death* (pamphlet), Society for Ethical Culture, 2 West 64th St., New York 23, N.Y.

12. Harry A. Overstreet, *The Mature Mind,* New York, Norton, 1949.

13. Erich Fromm, *The Sane Society,* New York, Rinehart and Company, 1955.

14. Rollo May, *Man's Search for Himself,* New York, Norton, 1953.

15. James Agee, *A Death in the Family,* New York, McDowell, Oblensky, Inc., 1958(?)

APPENDIX V

1. Emil Durkheim, *The Elementary Forms of Religious Life,* New York, Macmillan Company, 1926.

2. Bronislaw Malinowski, *Magic, Science and Religion and Other Essays,* Boston, Beacon Press, 1948.

3. Eliot Dismore Chapple and Carleton Stevens Coon, *Principles of Anthropology,* New York, Henry Holt and Company, 1942.

4. Arnold L. Van Gennep, *Les Rites de Passage,* Paris, Librairie Critique, 1909.

Advertising, 50
Affection, show of, 15, 100, 102
Affectation of undertakers, 95
Anthropological theories, 172-175
Associations of funeral directors: Advertising, 99, 131; Jewish, 98; National, 97-99; Negro, 98; Selected Morticians, 98
Attendance, 21, 24, 124, 137
Attitudes toward death, 1-7, 53, 70, 72, 123
Aversion to bodies and the funeral director, 15, 31, 71-75, 131

Bargaining, family and undertaker, 29-54, 66, 67, 115, 119, 130, 131, 147
Bereavement, 8-10; fatigue, 23-25; strains, 146; insight, 141-146
Body, disposal of, 53, 54, 69, 135, 150; treatment of, 75
Business (including supply houses), 35, 78, 80, 81, 85, 87, 89-108, 116, 131, 133, 159

Catholic groups, 19, 119, 138, 167
Children, reaction to death, 2, 169-171
Church funeral societies, 134-136
Cities, small, and rural communities, 13, 20, 60, 72, 75, 95, 112, 114, 115, 119, 124, 146
City civilization, effects of, 21, 24, 72, 84, 112-128, 137, 144, 150
Commercial influences, dominance of, 89-108
Committal service, 24, 25, 66, 123, 124
Communication, 115
Community aspects, 28, 115, 126, 127, 146, 147
Community provision, 133, 155-158
Conflicts, public, clergy and undertakers, 67-70
Contributions to causes, 69, 135
Cooperative funeral societies, 42, 108, 131-133
Costs, 39-54, 59, 61, 137, 147
Cremation, 69, 118, 130, 135, 136, 150, 166-168
Culture, role of, 14, 25, 140 ff., 144-146

Church, role of, 18, 21-24, 110, 116, 150

Design, series of gatherings, 9, 31, 34, 69

Embalming, 69, 78, 117, 119, 130, 150
Essentials of funeral, 148-155
Extravagance, 23, 45, 94, 100, 102, 121, 128, 130, 137, 145
Eyes, bequest to Eye-Bank, 137-139, 150, 161-163, 165

Family, 8, 23, 120, 122, 127, 146
Fraternal orders and veterans' groups, 19, 69, 116
Functions, 119-128
Funeral directors: attitudes, 42, 65, 72, 101, 103, 108, 119; career, 85-88; competence, 36-42, 82, 111; ethics, 35, 46, 51, 57, 58, 81, 104, 105, 129; isolation, 52, 59, 61, 83, 89, 147; "joiners," 35, 76; relations to clergy, 61-70; to government agencies, 57-60; to physicians, 55, 56; to settlement workers, 129, 130; to social work, 57, 60, 61; role in community, 71-88, 103; services, 14, 21-24, 37-39, 53, 54, 57, 60, 69; values, 159
Funeral establishment, 17, 20, 36, 47, 72-77, 86, 95, 114, 117, 118, 130

Grief, 9, 15, 31, 130, 141
Group aspects, 5, 122-124, 126, 144, 152
Guilt, 15, 33, 170

Historical changes, 112-119, 129-131, 147
Humor, 5, 6, 19

Immigrant groups, 84, 115, 116, 120
Insight into ultimate values, 94, 120, 122, 123, 126-128, 137, 141, 144, 145, 147
Interaction, 19, 22, 25, 126, 127

Jewish aspects, 98, 99, 115, 119, 167

Labor, efforts of, 134

Licensing, 59, 75, 105, 133
Lobbying, 104, 131-133

Medical school, bequest of body to, 137-139, 161, 162, 164, 165
"Memory image," 12, 52
Methods of author, 27, 28, 109-111, 140, 141

Organizational structure, national, 89, 96-103; discipline, 104-108

Pressures on family and undertaker, 34-36, 54, 136, 137
Private enterprise, 106-108
Professional status, claim to, 77-83, 103
Prominent person, 124-126, 137
Public enterprise and government regulation, 42, 106-108, 131, 132
Public opinion, 40, 41, 81, 82, 103
Public relations, 103

Racial discrimination, 87, 95, 98
Remains, emphasis on, 64, 96, 100, 111, 147
Responsibilities: on the family, 2, 12-14, 29, 127; on the undertaker, 29, 30, 38, 56
"Restoration" of facial features, 88, 117, 119
Return home, 25, 26
Revelrous behavior, 18, 19, 123
Roman Catholics, 138, 161

Secular gatherings, 136, 137
Service, the, 10, 21-24, 66
Solace, 41, 82, 110
Status, 24, 102, 120-122, 127, 131, 137
Study commissions, 159, 160

Trade journals, 100
Training schools, 105
Trends and experiments, 129-139

Wake, the, 16-22, 69, 114, 119, 146

ABOUT THE AUTHOR

LeRoy Bowman was born into circumstances that early in life prepared him for objective appraisal of social and religious ceremonies. Of mixed German-English parentage, one of a family of moderate means, living in a neighborhood of recent immigrants in a semi-rural area of a small town, he found his curiosity aroused by the conflicts of customs and beliefs and the differences in values held by intimate and friendly neighbors. It was, therefore, not a new experience, but a flowering of old interests, later in life, to take charge of settlement activities among peoples of diverse racial and national origins in Chicago, Brooklyn, and Manhattan. In these places he had deep sympathy with the deprivations of the poor, the driving need for recognition, and the compelling force of cultural pressures that, combined, resulted in extravagant birth, marriage, and death observances.

Impelled partly by interest in these rites, more largely by economic necessity in straightened circumstances, he earned his room rent in college for two years by sleeping in an undertaker's parlor to receive emergency calls, and by assisting in some of the work of preparing bodies for burial. At first with fear and later with indifference, he slept within ten feet of the "slumber room" where bodies often lay awaiting the last ceremony.

With a strong religious bent, he enrolled in a divinity school, became president of a pre-ministerial group of prospective clergymen, and received training in an out-of-the-way church at a rural crossroads in Indiana. But the pull of interest in social conditions, social processes, and social causes was too great; he gave up any idea of the ministry to devote himself to social studies, social amelioration, and reform.

In college teaching his earliest curiosity in the customs of various peoples was again aroused by the contrast between the anthropologists' analysis of the significance of the funeral in primitive societies and the neglect of the subject by other social scientists dealing with urban, industrial society. This book is in large part an effort to satisfy that curiosity by the application of scientific methods in the first part of the study and the use of a combined philosophical and practical approach in the last chapter.